# Four Voices,
# Four Continents

How we Eluded Hitler, Survived Stalin,

Made a Life in Africa,

and Finally Arrived in America

ADA MOSZKOWSKI HARRISON

SOFIA MOSZKOWSKI FREER

**BEBO Press**

Cover design by Jessica Reed

ISBN-13: 978-0-9995956-0-2

# DEDICATION

This book is dedicated to our children and grandchildren.

# CONTENTS

# PROLOGUE

Setting the stage for a family story of survival in four voices

Mother and Father on their honeymoon, 1929

We are the daughters of Arthur and Dora Mozskowski. This is the tale of our journey during and after World War II, beginning when we fled Poland in 1939, under Hitler's Luftwaffe aerial assault. Ours is not a typical Holocaust escape story. Our father's position as an engineer afforded us a path that was not possible for many Jews. Although we endured life-threatening hardships during our long journey, we avoided the concentration camps where six million Jews perished. An incredible number of coincidences, thanks to both our father's efforts and luck, allowed our family to survive the war and eventually immigrate to the United States in 1950.

We were both living in the San Francisco Bay Area when we rediscovered two audiotapes our father had recorded in Polish shortly before his death in 1975. These tapes were the impetus that drove us to write this story. We felt compelled to preserve, for our American-born children and grandchildren, Father's personal accounts of Hitler's invasion of Poland and the conditions in a Soviet labor camp.

We are the only living witnesses to each other's past life, so different from the lives we have now. Our parents' voices predominate in the early years of the family saga. Ada (Dunia), who was nine when the war began, lends a child's perspective; Sofia (Zosia), who was only two, was too young to remember much of those early turbulent war years.[1] We devote some of our story to Józia (pronounced "yu-zha") Łaszczyk, our housekeeper and nanny before the war, and a pillar of support and source of comfort during our darkest hours.

---

[1] Zosia is a conventional Polish nickname for Sofia, but Dunia is not a conventional nickname for Ada. Nobody is quite sure where Ada's nickname came from, but it stuck.

We made every attempt to make a literal translation of Father's tapes because we wanted our father's practicality and matter-of-fact, man-of-few-words personality to come through. To fill in gaps in Father's account and in our childhood memories, we took the liberty of quoting passages from our mother's memoirs.[2] Thus began this family history in four voices.

Because Mother's memoirs are, themselves, a completed text (bound and housed at several Holocaust museums), we decided not to include her entire manuscript here. Instead, we include those portions that interweave Mother's voice with ours to fill out the family story. All excerpts from Mother's memoirs appear in italics to differentiate them from the other voices.

Our chapters' chronology is rough, as must be the case when four storytellers, over the course of decades, recount their memories. Working with our parents' account of our journey from Poland through Asia and Africa, together with our editors' research, we constructed a map showing the most likely path on this route:

Radom, Poland
Lublin, Poland
Czortków, Poland
Tavda, Russia
Samarkand, Uzbekistan, USSR
Kermine, Uzbekistan, USSR
Krasnovodsk, USSR
Pahlavi, Iran
Tehran, Iran

---

[2] "Dora Gross Moszkowski: Life Story" (self-published, 1987)

Ahwaz, Iran

Bandar Shapur, Iran

Karachi, India

Mombasa, Kenya

Tengeru, Tanganyika

Dar es Salaam, Tanganyika

Johannesburg, South Africa

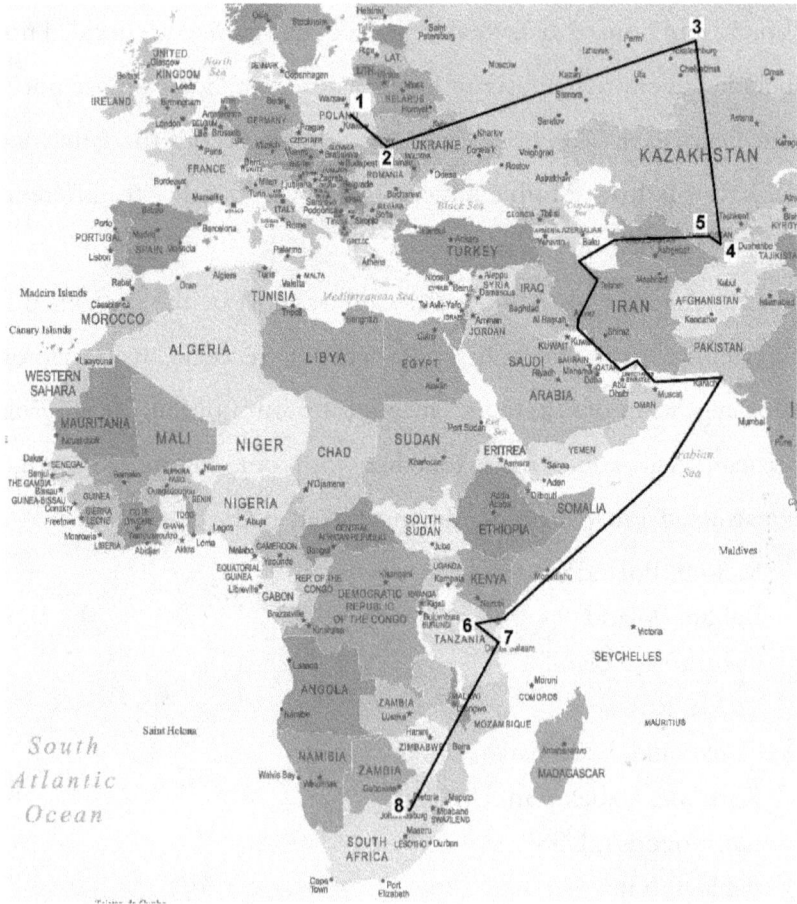

Approximate route, with locations where the family stayed for longer than a brief stopover: 1. Radom, 2. Czortków, 3. Tavda, 4. Samarkand, 5. Kermine, 6. Tengeru, 7. Dar es Salaam, 8. Johannesburg.

Throughout the story, we use location names that existed at that time in history, including Polish names for the cities that belonged to Poland at the time. Much of the region through which we traveled in our journey to Russia is now part of Ukraine. Czortków, Poland is now listed as Chortkiv, Ukraine on English language maps, and Lwów is Lviv, Ukraine.

Several locations have changed names in the decades since we were there. Kermine has been known as Navoi since 1958. Pahlavi is now the port of Anzali, known as Bandar Anzali. The "Iranian port" that Father mentions is most likely Bandar Imam Kohmeini, which was known as Bandar Shapur before the Iranian Revolution in 1979. Krasnovodsk, once part of the USSR, is in the country of Turkmenistan. Karachi was in India at the time, as the country of Pakistan did not yet exist. The country of Tanzania was known as Tanganyika when we lived there.

Ada Moszkowski Harrison

Sofia Moszkowski Freer

January 2018

# 1. ESCAPE FROM HITLER:
## FATHER'S TAPE THAT STARTED IT ALL

On September 3, 1939, German bombs started falling on Radom, Poland, where the family had been living for the previous year.

Mother, Dunia, and Zosia in pre-war Poland

I begin on September 3, 1939, at the moment my wife and daughters [and Józia] left Radom, heading toward Lublin. I watched as the truck pulled away. I was left alone and I had many problems. My first task was to go to Warsaw to bring back some essential supplies for the factory that were not available in Radom.[3] Polish military authorities allowed me to use the company car, but wartime conditions would make the trip extremely difficult.

I was able to obtain a special pass from military headquarters. On the pass it was written that Engr. Artur Moszkowski[4] was traveling to Warsaw on military matters and that all military and civilian personnel were to assist him in the execution of his assignment. Accompanied by a clerk from the company, I proceeded north to Warsaw [65 miles].

At the beginning, the trip was uneventful. Then we heard German planes and watched as they strafed two police vehicles on the road ahead of us. We heard bombs and machine gun fire. We saw many bodies on the ground. The police stopped our car and ordered us to take a wounded man to the hospital in Radom. They placed the wounded man in the back seat, a policeman sat with him, and another policeman got into the front passenger seat. There was no room in the car for the clerk; I had to leave him by the roadside. So, using up precious time and gasoline, I drove back to Radom, and after leaving the wounded man and the policeman at the hospital, resumed my trip to Warsaw. I picked up the clerk from where I had left him on the

[3] Father was chief engineer of a munitions factory in Radom (Kromoloski).

[4] Artur is the Polish spelling of Father's name; when Mother refers to him she uses the English, Arthur.

road. The Germans made our journey to Warsaw interesting. Several times they flew overhead bombing the road, and we had to abandon our car to hide in ditches by the side of the road. In this fashion, we finally reached Warsaw. The city was relatively calm in spite of sporadic bombardment.

The clerk and I found a hotel room. That night, soldiers came to our door commanding that all able-bodied men go with them so that they could be put to work on defense fortifications and shelters for Warsaw. My pass exempted me from this order, but the clerk had to comply. He came back in the morning relating how he was taken from place to place, but no work materialized. Finally we were able to obtain our supplies.

But how to get back to Radom? Because of the extra trip to the hospital in Radom, we did not have enough gas. My pass from the military allowed me to get gas, but it was not available until the following morning. That evening I was permitted to make a phone call to the factory and was told that unless I could come right away, there was no point in returning. The Germans were just outside of town, and were expected to occupy Radom during the night. At that point we decided to drive to Lublin.

In the morning we drove across the Vistula River to fill up with gas. From then on, our progress was very slow. The road was packed with people leaving Warsaw. There were people on foot, in handcarts, on bicycles, and in cars. A few military vehicles were also on the road. A mile or two took hours.

Then suddenly there was panic. People were running off the road to hide in ditches, as German airplanes strafed the roadway. I took advantage of this. As soon as the road was clear, I stepped on the gas and tore down the road at maximum speed. In this fashion we arrived in Minsk Mazowiecki, the next town on the way to Lublin, where I hoped to be reunited with my family. In Minsk I had a flat tire which took 15-20 minutes to repair.

As we neared the next town, Siedlice, we saw that it was in flames. A man coming down the road from Siedlice told us that twenty minutes earlier the Germans, using incendiary bombs, had burned the city to the ground. If not for the flat tire, we would have been there right in the middle of the bombardment! As we drove on, we found the road filled with rubble, fallen telephone poles, etc., but somehow we managed to get through. Then we came to a small river where the bridge had been destroyed. What now? After a moment's hesitation, I just went ahead and drove across the river.

Several hours later, when we were but a few miles from Lublin, we were forced to stop. Up to now my pass got us through police and army checkpoints.[5] But here, so close to my destination, the pass did not work. I didn't understand why I was not allowed into Lublin. Later, I learned that the president of Poland, Ignacy Mościcki, had fled Warsaw and was hiding out in Lublin. Entry into town was blocked to ensure his safety. I wasn't about to be stopped now! I simply turned left onto a narrow country lane, traveled parallel to the highway for a few kilometers, and returned to the main road. With no further

---

[5] At this point, Father was obviously no longer on a military mission.

checkpoints or mishaps, we arrived in Lublin. I dropped off my companion. As I neared my sister's house in Lublin, I saw my two daughters playing in the front yard and I broke down completely. All my strength was exhausted.

After a few hours of rest and sleep, I was finally reunited with my wife; she did not witness my return, having been away on a visit with my mother, aunt, and cousin.

We remained in Lublin for several days while bombs fell and buildings went up in flames. With the Germans on the outskirts of town I decided that the only way to save ourselves was to leave. I wanted to take my whole family, including my mother, but she refused to leave. Having survived WWI, she believed that Hitler would not harm women or children. "You go" she said "but leave your wife and daughters with me. It will be less risky for all." Against my mother's advice, I refused to leave without my family.

We left during the night, since daytime travel was not possible. On the way we stopped in Lwów for a few hours, and as we were leaving we came under German artillery fire. We managed to get away under a hail of bullets. On the way from Lwów to Tarnopol we got another unpleasant surprise. All car drivers, without exception, were directed to drive off the road onto a field. We were all told to leave our vehicles and go on foot to a nearby village where we were likely to remain for the duration of the war. I was determined to continue on our journey. In the evening, with the help of a young man who was my sister's employee, I pushed the car back onto the road. Then I turned on the engine, pushed the gas pedal to the floor, and with lights off, took off down the road. "Stop or we will shoot," they yelled after us. They commenced shooting, but it was dark, and their shots missed us.

We drove to Czortków, where we met many acquaintances who had also eluded Hitler by fleeing east. Since it was the day before the Jewish New Year, we decided to stay in Czortków during the holiday while the car was in repair. On September 16 we decided to continue our journey,[6] but returnees from the east told us that the Russians had already cut off all roads in and out of Czortków.

After occupying the city, the Russians ordered all engineers to register with them. They needed engineers for rebuilding bridges and other projects. Since I knew some Russian, they immediately hired me to rebuild a bombed-out bridge. On the basis of this experience I was advised to report to the Department of Bridges in Lwów, to rebuild other bombed out bridges, tunnels, etc. In Lwów I stayed with a cousin, and every weekend I went to Czortków to see my family for a few short hours. This arrangement lasted for almost a year; I in Lwów, my wife in Czortków. Then came a time when the Russians decided to offer Russian passports to all refugees from the west. I applied for the passport but my wife absolutely refused to do so. We didn't take passports and as a result I was laid off from my job. I returned to Czortków.[7]

---

[6] Our original escape plan was to drive across the Romanian border and eventually make our way through the Balkans to Palestine, following the path of thousands of other Jews.

[7] Father's first tape ends in Czortków. The second tape begins in Russia. The intervening events are chronicled in Mother's writing and Dunia's recollections.

# 2. MY FATHER, THE HERO: DUNIA'S EARLY YEARS IN PRE-WAR POLAND

When Dunia reflects on her prewar childhood, her stories are remarkable for their innocence and their ordinariness: they capture a world when childhood itself was still possible.

Father and Dunia in the 1930s

As I listened to Father telling his story into the tape recorder at his breakfast table, I shook in wonder and disbelief. I had always known his bravery and chutzpah defied imagination. With amazing luck, quick thinking, and a series of coincidences, he saved his own life and later ours many times over. He didn't let anything stand in his way; his determination, perseverance, and resourcefulness were unbelievable. I am quite sure that if it weren't for our father, we would not have survived the many crises and life and death experiences during those early war years. He was always a "doer." He welcomed and overcame many challenges with an optimistic outlook and a fearless demeanor.

I always admired and worshipped my father. I was also afraid of him and terrified of disappointing him. He had high expectations and was a strict disciplinarian. He was strong and steadfast and had little tolerance for weakness. When I cried, he called me a "soft egg," a disparaging remark. He wanted me to be strong and unafraid, but I was mostly a coward, afraid to stand up to him. Zosia was able to, and he admired her for it.

Father's risk-taking behavior was also evident in choices that endangered our safety. One of my earliest memories (at about four years of age) was a Sunday afternoon outing outside of Krakow, Poland with my parents and paternal grandmother. On the way home we tried to board an overcrowded bus. The bus driver told Father that there was no more room, but Father wouldn't take no for an answer. He grabbed me under his arm and jumped on the bus step as the driver pulled away. We were thrown to the pavement. I remember people yelling, "they must be dead." We were not dead, of course, but I had a big bump on my forehead and was in a lot of pain. That was not the last time he pulled such a stunt. Zosia later had a similar experience.

Before the war broke out, by the time I was nine, Father managed to teach me how to ride a bicycle, swim, ice skate, and ski. These were no mean feats, as he had to overcome both my Mother's fears and mine. The bicycle became an important connection between me and my father. I remember the joy I experienced when the two of us would ride into the country and leave Mother behind.

The summer I was seven, we were on vacation in a village where we had rented a villa. One morning, Father and I rode our bikes to the train station to meet my aunt who was coming to visit. Suddenly a drunken man on a bicycle ran into me, and I fell against his still spinning spokes, which tore a hole in my upper thigh. The only way to get back to the village was to ride there. I was bleeding and in pain, but Father made me get back on the bike, and with his encouraging comments about my bravery ("curka zuch" – brave daughter in Polish) I rode back to town, where a local doctor sewed it up without anesthesia. The wound got infected, and I have the scar to this day.

My earliest memories go back to age four. We were staying with my paternal grandmother in Krakow, in her one-bedroom apartment overlooking the railroad. I would fall asleep to the sound of the trains, and I have enjoyed the sound of train whistles and the chugging locomotives ever since. I slept in my grandmother's room, Mother slept on a day bed in the dining room, and Józia slept in the kitchen. Even though Grandmother had indoor plumbing, she still had a chamber pot under her bed, which I found fascinating.

Father, who was looking for work in the city, visited on weekends to be with us. I once greeted him at the door with, "What did you bring me?" to which he replied that if that was the most important thing for me, next time he would send a gift but would not come himself. Of course, I begged him to come, and never again asked for a present.

When he was there, Father played games with me and made doll furniture out of old postcards. When I was a little older, Father started a stamp collection, ostensibly for me, which I have to this day. He loved collecting stamps, and it caused an ongoing conflict between my parents (Mother wanted the money for more practical things.) I remember when we were in Russia years later, Father bought some stamps when Mother needed a coat. He thought that the Russian stamps would become really valuable; they never did.

One of my early memories at age four or five is being on some kind of ranch with my mother and several other mothers and children. We had some fun activities and outings. One day, as we were coming back from an outing, my father showed up, having come to take us home. He met us on the road, and for some inscrutable reason, I not only ignored Father but actually denied knowing him! Understandably he was hurt and angry. I cried in remorse all the way home, but for the life of me I could not explain or figure out why I did this.

After Father got a permanent job in Katowice, we moved there for the next four years. We had a four-room apartment. One was Father's room, which also served as the family dining room; one was Mother's; one was mine, and one was Zosia's after she was born. Only my room had a bed; the others had pull-out sofas. Mother did not like the look of beds, for some reason. Many years later she told me that sleeping in separate bedrooms was actually more romantic. It also may have been the style in those years. All of Mother's furniture came from Scandinavia, and since there was no payment on credit, the pieces were delivered when there was money for them. The last piece was delivered just before the war.

One of the daily morning rituals was getting a cold sponge bath; I would stand on a stool in the bathroom, and Mother would sponge me down with cold tap water. Afterward I would swallow a tablespoon of cod liver oil. I hated both, but they were supposed to have an immunizing effect. The ritual seems to have worked, because I rarely caught colds. On the rare occasions when I did get sick, Mother hovered over my bed with a worried look on her face, and paced the floor nervously, expecting the worst. She also catered to my every whim on those occasions, but I still preferred Father's cheerful presence and playing games with him.

Father usually worked at his desk every evening, Mother went to her frequent meetings, and I was lonely. Once I saw the janitor's family all seated at a table in the evening, and I asked my parents if we all could just live in one room.

I was not an outgoing or adventurous child. For instance, when I was in the park with Mother or Józia and saw strange children approaching to ask me to play, I would hide behind the park bench to avoid having to face them. I was afraid that they might ask me to play a game I did not know, or that their rules might be different. With my own friends I enjoyed many indoor and outdoor games. I preferred playing with boys because their games were more interesting, but when they started getting rough I would run off. Girls liked to set up doll tea parties etc., but then it got boring.

One of the games I played with boys was "war." We drew a circle on the ground, divided it into countries, and threw a penknife into the opponent's territory. If it stuck, we could annex that part for ourselves. (In retrospect, it is not surprising that in Poland, a country that had undergone many divisions and partitions, this kind of game would be popular.)

In the summer, my parents rented a cottage or a villa in the country, and we stayed there the whole summer, with Father commuting on weekends to be with us. I loved those vacations: bathing in the nearby river, building dams on little streams, playing with my friends, swimming in the public pool, gathering shells along the river bank. Once two of my friends and I had the ingenious idea of gathering flowers and vegetables from nearby gardens, loading them in our wagon, and trying to sell them to neighbors. When our parents found out, we had to return the money and the goods and apologize. Still, it was fun while it lasted.

The summer after I turned seven, we were on vacation when I noticed that Mother did not come swimming with us or even go in the water. When I asked about it, I was told that the doctor told her not to go swimming. I left it at that until the end of summer vacation when I asked again, fully expecting to be told, "We already explained it to you." Instead, to my great surprise, they told me that I was going to have a little brother or sister soon! When we returned home, a little friend told me that my mother was going to have a baby. I was shocked. How did she know? I thought it was a family secret. She said: "Look at your mother's big belly!" I went home, and for the first time noticed Mother's protruding stomach!

I had learned early in life not to see things I was not supposed to see. There were many things I was not supposed to see, like Mother's smoking. When I was in preschool I saw boys going to the bathroom, so I saw their genitals. I wasn't supposed to see genitals, smoking, pregnancy. I still don't notice certain things until someone points them out and calls them by name.

Two months later, on October 11, 1937, Zosia was born. I was not thrilled. A little sister was not on my list of priorities. A big brother would have been nice (though I guess I knew by then that was not possible) or a puppy, but what does one do with a little sister? On the morning she was being born (at home) I wrapped my favorite doll in a baby bunting and gave it to Mother, hoping she would be satisfied. I was then sent to stay with family friends who, upon learning that I had a baby sister, started congratulating me, to which I replied, "Don't congratulate me; it's not my fault."

When I returned home, I found an ugly, red baby on my bed! My reaction was to announce that I guessed I wasn't needed there anymore, whereupon I turned on my heel and started to walk out. Father intercepted my flight and brought me back. The reason they put the baby on my bed was that there was no crib for Zosia, due to Mother's superstition that it was bad luck to prepare things for the baby, in case it dies. This was never verbalized, of course, but since infant survival was not assured at that time, there was some reality to that fear.

Once Zosia was no longer occupying my bed, I realized that she was a beautiful baby, and my sisterly feelings were aroused when I experienced jealousy at her smiling at my friends. She was MY sister and the smiles should be for me.

Shortly after she was born, Father looked at Zosia and declared, "Ona dam nam szkole," Polish for "She will teach us a lesson." Mother, however, told me that from now on I would have to watch my step because Zosia would want to imitate everything I did. Fortunately, Zosia was too smart for that. Incidentally, I always said that I had named her, because I liked the name Zosia. But Father claimed that it was his idea, so he would have children "from A to Z."

My sister was not only beautiful, but really smart and precocious. At 20 months of age, when hearing a calf low, she observed that "little moo is crying for its mommy," and a short time later in a boat on the river Vistula she concluded that it wasn't pee-pee (as all liquids were called), but a "big water." Her deductive reasoning even at that age was phenomenal.

We used to take the train to our aunt's house in Lublin for Passover. I loved my aunt (father's sister) but did not like her husband. Much later, I found out that nobody else in the family liked him either. My aunt made the most delicious chocolate rum balls, which she kept in a secret drawer. She would call me over with a conspiratorial whisper, and offer me some. When Mother found out, she told my aunt, "don't spoil her," and for the longest time I thought that spoiling meant getting the rum balls, so I would ask my aunt: "Spoil me, auntie, spoil me." The Passover service was long and boring, and by the time the first dinner course arrived, I would be too tired and sleepy to enjoy it. After dinner, the service and singing continued late into the night, long after I was in bed. My "bed" was two large armchairs pushed together, large enough for me to lie in but too small to turn around. As the grownups became louder and louder, I could not sleep and kept calling Mother, who suggested that I tell myself a story. This worked well and became a lifelong habit, though sometimes the stories were so interesting that I hated to interrupt them and go to sleep.

For a long time I kept begging for a puppy, and finally my parents relented. We got a puppy and I was overjoyed, but my joy was short lived. The puppy was housebroken, and after a few hours started scratching at the front door, asking to be let out. My parents, knowing nothing about dogs, thought that he was trying to run away, so they locked the door. The poor puppy finally wet the floor, whereupon my parents decided he had to go. Crying all the way, I walked with Józia to return the puppy. I did not own another dog until thirty years later, when my youngest daughter asked for one.

My early education was sporadic. I attended preschool while we were living with my grandmother in Krakow. I still remember some of the songs and games we played. There were no kindergartens in Poland. When I was six, my mother organized a home school based on the philosophy of Maria Montessori. Mother gathered three other families, and they hired a teacher who came to our house every day. I remember being fascinated by her approach to teaching reading and writing and I thoroughly enjoyed the process. At the end of the school year I had to take an exam at a public school before I could advance to the next year. In this way I completed first and second grades.

At age seven, I disappointed Father. He had tried to teach me advanced math by giving me algebraic exercises which I somehow learned to solve. However, during the end-of-year exam between first and second grades, I said I did not know how much was twelve minus eight. Somehow, I passed, but on the way home Father kept on saying "my daughter didn't know twelve minus eight." I cried all the way home, and to this day when I stumble on a subtraction problem, numbers twelve, eight, and four are always involved.

When I was eight, we moved to Radom and I started third grade in a private Jewish school. The school was fine, but I hated having to walk to school on Sunday when everybody else, it seemed, was dressed up and going to church. (Schools in Poland ran six days a week, so the Jewish school was off on Saturday.) My fourth-grade year was in Czortków during the war.

Once I learned to read, reading became my favorite pastime. I read many books that were translated into Polish from English: *Emil and the Detectives, Bambi, Heidi, Adventures of Tom Sawyer,* and *Huckleberry Finn,* and later all the books by L.M. Montgomery, starting with *Anne of Green Gables,* which I had practically memorized. Incidentally, when reading about Tom's and Huck's adventures, I remember thinking I was glad I was a girl, so I didn't have to do all those daring and scary things.

In the third grade in Radom, I had my first "romance" with a boy named Marek, who slobbered me with puppy kisses during a school play that we attended together. For Mothers' Day we put on our own play. I was cast as a mother with three children, two daughters plus Marek as my little boy. The girls were to give me presents, but Marek was to say that he had nothing to give me but love, and give me a kiss. When we rehearsed in class, the other kids snickered, so the kiss was postponed until the actual day of the performance.

Since it was to be a surprise for our mothers, the teacher, who had no children of her own, took me to a hairdresser for a wave set and dressed me in someone's long skirt and blouse. My mother wasn't just surprised when she saw me; she was shocked. Marek's mother dressed him in a royal velvet suit and sprayed him with cologne. He looked like little Lord Fauntleroy, and to me he looked and smelled like a sissy. All my affection for him evaporated at that moment. The play itself was a disaster. When Marek came on stage and saw our whole class assembled in front, snickering in anticipation, he broke into tears and ran off the stage with the rest of the "cast" following. Thus ended my theatrical debut and my romance.

My parents were a product of their generation and status in society. My father's family was middle class. My father was the younger of two children; his sister was some three years older. Their parents were divorced, which was quite rare for the time and circumstances. From the little that he told us, both his parents found him hard to handle, and he was passed back and forth from one to the other. For example, when they tried to discipline him for tormenting his sister, he told them that for every spanking he got, he would administer the same to his sister. Even though I don't remember my paternal grandfather (he died when I was three), I was told that he was a cold man who never showed any affection for his own children but apparently showered me with love when I was a baby. I remember my grandmother as a rather stiff and proper lady.

My mother was also one of two children, with a brother who was seven years older. Her family was poor, as apparently her father had no ability to support his family.[8] He was also chronically depressed, having never gotten over losing his wife at an early age. My maternal grandmother contracted a fatal case of dysentery after caring for an ill neighbor. My mother was only eighteen years old at the time. My mother described her mother as an angel who sacrificed herself for others, and she grieved for her for many years.

One thing Grandmother did was to save every penny to pay for Mother's education, ostensibly so her brother would not be ashamed of her. (High school education was free for boys only.) Education became my mother's exit visa out of poverty and her ticket to independence. She worked hard, overcoming many obstacles and achieved the highest honor: a PhD degree. Being a professional was glorified, and made her "somebody"; being a mother did not.

At that time in Poland women hired nannies for the children; taking care of children was not a high priority, especially among educated women. Children's feelings were of no consequence. What mattered was that they behave, do well in school, do as they were told, respect their parents, and make their parents proud.

---

[8] According to Mother's memoirs, her father worked at an insurance company for little pay. He was a religious man who believed that "God would provide."

In my family, punishment involved lectures from Mother and the silent treatment from Father. Mother would tell me that a good daughter (which I obviously was not) would act and respond in an acceptable way. I hated that fictitious good daughter who somehow always said and did precisely what Mother expected. Father's silent treatment could go on for weeks and would end only with my apology (at Mother's insistence) for deeds I either did not remember or was not sorry for. From time to time all of us were victims of the silent treatment, during which time the person singled out was treated as if she did not exist. When Mother was the victim, a pall would fall on the whole family.

My parents did not fight or argue, but they often engaged in spirited political discussions, as they were often on opposite sides of the political spectrum. The raised voices on those occasions certainly sounded like fighting. When they disagreed on non-political matters, they would place bets as to who was right. I remember walking a long distance on a hot afternoon in search of an outdoor thermometer to settle the bet as to the temperature at that time.

# 3. DEPORTATION AND LIFE IN RUSSIA: DUNIA AND MOTHER

Hundreds of thousands of Polish citizens were deported to slave labor camps in Siberia after Russia invaded Poland in 1940. Our family was among the few Jews deported.

Sketch supplied courtesy of The General Sikorski Memorial House in Glasgow. Used with permission.

*In February 1940 the Russians started deportations to Siberia. The first deportees were the Polish members of the legal and law-enforcement professions. In April they deported wealthy landowners and businessmen. Both of these groups were residents of eastern Poland, then under Russian rule. Our situation was different because we came from the western part of Poland, then under German occupation and thus were "safe" according to my colleagues.*

*However, at midnight, the 28th of June 1940, there was a knock on our door. We opened it, and three armed Russian men entered.*

◻    ◻    ◻

I remember that day in June. Russian authorities had announced that there would be an air raid drill at night. They ordered a blackout. The whole town was to be completely dark; we had to cover our windows so no light would shine through. Then, under cover of complete darkness, they came to deport us. Three armed soldiers came into our rented room and ordered us to pack our belongings. There was no explanation as to what was going on or where they were taking us. I was so scared that I had to go to the bathroom several times, and each time a soldier with a gun stood outside the bathroom door. This made me even more nervous. Did they think I was communicating with someone outside?

Two-year-old Zosia was sound asleep in her crib. One soldier, older and more kindly than the others, turned to Mother and whispered, "Bring the little bed and some warm milk for her." It was fortunate that Father had lost his job in Lwów and we were all together when they came for us. They deported those who were at home. Many families were separated: husbands from wives, children from parents.

◻        ◻        ◻

*We were taken by truck to the railway station. Simultaneously, many trucks arrived at the station. The sun was already high on the horizon. The local people, had heard about our impending deportation, arrived at the station and stood on the other side of a fence. When they saw us getting into the train they threw bread, rolls, cakes, candies, and cookies to us over the fence.*

◻        ◻        ◻

As we were being herded like cattle into the freight cars, we came close to being separated from Józia. Single people were ordered to remain behind. Later, we found that they were destined for prison camps, instead of the labor camps where families were sent. Father stepped forward, claimed Józia as his cousin, and persuaded the soldiers to let her come with us.

◻        ◻        ◻

*Each box car had a sliding door and a platform on each side halfway up the wall. To reach the platform, we had to climb a ladder. In the floor was one big hole which we used as a toilet. About sixty people were crowded into each car. There were no windows. Some people slept on the floor and some on the platform. Zosia slept in the little crib which we were allowed to take with us from Czortków. Twice a day the door opened and we were given some soup and bread. Through cracks between the boards we could tell day from night. Our main concern was trying to find out which direction the train was going because we had no idea where we were being taken.*

◻        ◻        ◻

I was ten years old when we were put on the train to Tavda. The train was very hot, so I took off my shirt. I was fascinated by a twelve-year-old girl who wouldn't take off her shirt, and by two young men who were singing love songs in Polish. I still remember the words.

◻    ◻    ◻

*The journey lasted more than two weeks. A few times the train was stopped and we were let out for 10-15 minutes, and at least for this short time we could breathe some fresh air, and see the sun and sky. Our destination was a labor camp near a small town called Tavda in Sverdlosk province. A labor camp is not a prison or a concentration camp. We did not have barbed wire or guards. We were free to move around the camp but could not leave without the written permission from the camp commandant, and we had to observe the curfew. The most burdensome feature was the forced labor. In the center of the camp was a small store with meager provisions, like salt and bread; sugar was available once a month. People had to wait hours to get bread that looked and tasted like clay.*

◻    ◻    ◻

In Tavda, all Polish school children were placed in one of three grades, according to age. I, who should have been a fourth grader, was placed in the second grade. Older students, including teenagers, were placed in the third grade. None of us knew any Russian, and all instruction was in Russian. Somehow, I picked up the language in a short time, as did most of the others. I remember that by the time our family was moved to a different location within the camp, my Russian was quite fluent and Polish and Russian children attended classes together. We interacted easily, and at recess we all played together.

When we first arrived, we received care packages from friends in Poland. These supplemented our meager food rations. But there were many weeks and months when we had little to eat. Józia and I, as well as other refugees, planted potatoes; often that was the only food we had. One of my duties was to get bread, which was often in short supply. I had to wait in a long line before the store opened, at which time people would rush in to purchase the precious commodity. More than once I was pushed and shoved by larger, stronger adults, and occasionally I returned to the barracks in tears, empty-handed. Only working people were eligible for bread rations, according to the Russian slogan "who doesn't work, doesn't eat."

✿    ✿    ✿

*We stayed in barracks which had already been prepared for us. Each family, regardless of size, got one room with cooking facilities. As far as I remember, the number of deportees in our transport was about one thousand. The first order of the camp commandant was that all men, except the very old, had to start working in a sawmill which was a short distance from the camp. They were paid for their work. Women who had children could stay home. Arthur, who knew Russian and was an engineer, got a job as a foreman. I stayed home with the children. Our maid, Józia, who was still with us, had to go to work.*

*After about six months the situation changed.... We got a new commandant, a young sadistic type. His first task was to drive all women except the old ones to hard labor in the sawmill. The commandant did not force me to go to work, but one day he summoned me to his office. A strange dialogue ensued. He spoke Russian, which I understood to some extent; I answered in Polish. There was no interpreter because the talk was confidential. He told me I would not have to go to work if I followed his instructions, namely to visit people in their houses, listen to what they were talking about and report to him. That meant I was to be a spy. I pretended I did not understand. He repeated the offer a couple of times, and my answer was always the same, "I don't understand." He called me in the next day, and the scenario was repeated with one addition, "If you don't do what I want, I will send you to hard labor." At this point I told him that I was not going to work, because, according the Russian constitution, a mother with small children was allowed to stay home to take care of them. He started to yell, "You are a saboteur, and the punishment for a saboteur is prison!"*

*In the camp there was a small windowless hut adjacent to the commandant's office and connected to it by a door. It was used as a detention facility. Inside was only a bench and a bucket. This was the "prison" where I was confined. The first two days I was given some food, later only water. I spent four lonely days in complete darkness, sitting on the bench, with bed bugs crawling over me. I did not know whether it was day or night. Once a night, for four nights, a man opened the door of the jail and led me to the commandant's office. It was a huge room, and the glaring lights made me feel dizzy, especially after the darkness. The commandant asked only one question, "Are you going to work?" And my short answer was, "No." Then I was taken back to my cell. Every night my answer was the same. On the third night he threatened to send me far away so that I would never see my husband or children again. My answer again was that I was not going to do hard labor.... On the fifth day of my imprisonment I was not able to think logically. I did not feel anything. The hunger, freezing cold, exhaustion, and even the biting of the bed bugs did not bother me as much as before. The fifth night, when I was again brought into the office, all my convictions, my principles, and my fighting spirit were gone. This time he said that I would have to work only four hours a day. "Only four hours," he swore on the portrait of Stalin. In my state of mind, I capitulated. It was four o'clock in the morning when I came back to our room.... Two hours later the commandant came to escort me to the plant. He did it only for my sake because I did not understand Russian and he had a Russian questionnaire which I was to fill out. When we arrived at the plant, he talked with the officials, I suppose about me, and then he took my hand and physically forced me to pick up a piece of wood. As I learned later, this was a symbolic act showing that from now on I belonged to the plant.*

*My work began loading boards. After four hours, at noon, I started on my way home. I was stopped at the plant gate and told I could not leave. In my broken Russian I tried to explain that the commandant promised, swore, that I would work only four hours. I pleaded to no avail. I had to work eight hours. After a few weeks, the Russian workers decided, for patriotic reasons, to increase the working hours to twelve. There were two shifts. My faithful housekeeper, Józia, took upon herself the night shift in order to take care of the children while I worked days. My task was to load large boards into wheelbarrows and to unload them at another place. I was too weak to move the loaded wheelbarrow. I stood there, helpless, not knowing what to do. Three young Russian girls were working alongside of me. When one of them tried to help me, the others pulled her away, saying, "Whom are you helping? She had a better childhood than we did; let her suffer now."*

*Inside the plant was a train which picked up the lumber. On one occasion I was standing close to the railway tracks, and although I saw an oncoming train I was not able to move. A foreman pulled me away. He did not want to be responsible for losing a human life. I was transferred to a lighter job, collecting small pieces of wood and throwing then into a mill which ground them to sawdust. This task I had to perform twelve hours a day.*

◘    ◘    ◘

I remember a town hall meeting where the camp commandant was talking about Mother, mocking her. He demonstrated how "Moszkowskaya" would carry wood, beginning with three pieces and then dropping them until there was one. I remember feeling embarrassed for my mother. But generally, because Mother was depressed and sure that we would all die in Siberia, Józia took care of us.

Mother also worried about the relatives left behind. We had not received any word from them, and had no idea what was going on in Poland after Hitler's invasion. When Mother was depressed, I became anxious, and turned to Father for reassurance. I'll never forget his words; "You know Mother, she always worries. Next she'll be worrying about Stalin's health." Somehow to a ten-year-old this was not only hilarious, it was immeasurably comforting.

◘    ◘    ◘

*One day in May 1941, we received the good news that we were free! We could leave the camp. I quit the job immediately, but Arthur and Józia continued to work to earn a little more money. I enjoyed my freedom; I no longer needed a permit to go to town and could come and go at any time. I walked ostentatiously in front of the commandant's window, hoping he would see me."*

*The deportees started packing their few belongings and planning to leave Siberia for the recruiting centers in Uzbekistan.... The manager of the sawmill called Arthur into his office, offered to raise his salary, and tried to bribe him into staying. He took Arthur to a secret store filled with imported goodies such as caviar, ham, the best liqueurs and the most luxurious foodstuff reserved for the exclusive use of*

*Communist Party officials. The manager also warned Arthur about going to Uzbekistan because of the hot humid climate and contagious diseases, especially fatal for children…. "Do you want to kill your children?" he asked. In this respect, the manager was right. In Siberia, we had only two deaths, one little baby and a very old woman. But in Uzbekistan hundreds of Polish refugees died in the first few months, mostly of spotted typhus.[9] In spite of the warnings and the inducement to Arthur to stay, I insisted on leaving…. Arthur suggested that we stay for the winter; it was already September, and the Siberian winter had started. It was a logical suggestion, but… I was afraid that if we didn't take advantage of this opportunity, we would never be able to leave Siberia. On October 8, my birthday, I received the finest gift from my husband. He gave notice at work, and we could leave within two weeks. As we learned later, after January 1942 nobody was allowed to leave.*

---

[9] Mother refers to the illness as "spotted typhus," but there is no disease known by that name. In polish the name is tyfus plamisty, which means stained typhus. Two related illnesses are caused by bacteria from fleas, ticks, or rodents: typhus and spotted fever. Except for the quoted passages from Mother's memoirs, we call the disease typhus.

# 4. FROM RUSSIA TO AFRICA: FATHER'S SECOND TAPE

Father tells two different stories: one from Russia and another from Iran. In between, we have inserted Mother's story of the voyage from Uzbekistan.

Portrait of Father and Mother

In 1941 when Germany attacked Russia, our situation worsened. We had been deported to Siberia on the pretext of being German spies, and people, such as doctors and engineers who had found jobs in their professions, were laid off and forced to perform manual labor. This happened to me as well, even though the sawmill tried to retain me as an engineer. In the meantime a bridge, which was on the road to the sawmill, was completely washed out. It had to be rebuilt, but there was nobody to do the job. The labor camp commandant relieved me from my task of carrying lumber so I could rebuild the bridge. I was, however, required to carry an axe and work with my hands as a carpenter, even as I directed the rebuilding of the bridge.

The work of an engineer in Russia: We were supposed to rebuild this bridge that was almost completely destroyed. We took apart the superstructure until only the main supports remained. We barricaded the bridge at both ends so no one would fall in. During the night, a worker who was walking on the beams fell into the frozen river below and died. The director, his assistant, and I were held responsible. The incident could have led to dire consequences, such as prison or worse for all three of us. But because the director and his assistant were Russians, they were able to prove that they were not at fault. Witnesses were found who stated that the victim was seen walking along the beams during the day so he knew about the conditions of the bridge and thus the responsibility was his, and not ours. We all got off, but this illustrates how "safe" it was to be an engineer in Russia; one could be accused of anything and be subjected to severe punishment.

After the bridge work was completed, we got a so-called "amnesty," which freed us from the labor camps and permitted us to leave Tavda and go south.[10] We went to Samarkand, where I got a job in the city's building department without difficulty. My first assignment was to build a shelter for refugees from Dom. I was in charge of many who had come from labor prisons, and I was instructed to build a fence and watchtower so they couldn't escape. I started the project, but according to the blueprints from Moscow, we had to build a brick foundation. The problem was that there were no bricks; the company director promised to deliver them. In spite of all my efforts, phone calls, and written requests, I could not get any bricks. Excavations had been made in clay soil. When the rains came they were flooded and were rendered useless. In the meantime a Communist party official came to the building site to check on the progress. When I told him the problem, he said that my responsibility was to report the director to the regional administrative authority, and obtain the materials myself. If I did not do this, I would be guilty of sabotage, for which the punishment could be severe. At that time, I became ill with typhus, which in turn saved me from official repercussions.

It was characteristic of conditions in the Soviet Union that at the same time as I was working on the refugee shelter, I was also given an assignment to build a courtyard for a party official in town. This required many more bricks than the shelter. But in this case, all materials were made available without delay, and as a result, I was able

[10] On July 30, 1941, Stalin accepted a proposal from Polish General Sikorski to free the Poles who had been deported to Siberia. In exchange, they would form an army, under British command, to fight their mutual foe, Germany.

to complete the job ahead of schedule. Everything was there for party officials, nothing for refugees.

On the basis of the agreement between Stalin and General Sikorski, a Polish army was organized in the Soviet Union. All able-bodied men were accepted, with the exception of those who admitted to being Jews. I attempted to join the Polish army after we learned that those who enlisted would be allowed to leave Russia. They placed me in category A, but then rejected me because I was a Jew.

The first contingent was to leave Russia for the Middle East in March 1942. Since I was ill (with typhus), there was no possibility of attempting a departure at that time. The next transport was scheduled for August. What could we do? As before, only army personnel and their families would be allowed to leave. An acquaintance got us in touch with a sergeant in the Polish army, Ignacy Jerzyna, who agreed to list my wife as his sister, and me as his brother-in-law. Posing as Polish Catholics, we could join the army contingent. When we heard that the transport was due to leave, we packed our belongings and left Samarkand to go to the small town of Kermine where the Polish army was headquartered. It proved very difficult to make the trip.

◻   ◻   ◻

*Waiting for the train [in Tavda] Arthur noticed a shabby-looking man, and since we needed help with our baggage, Arthur approached him and offered to buy him a ticket...It turned out that the man, Alexander, was a big help to us during our long journey and in Uzbekistan.*

◻   ◻   ◻

Alexander managed to get hold of a truck, helped load our belongings, and drove us to the train station in spite of a high malarial fever which forced him to stay behind. The trains and the station were so overcrowded that we could not even get onto the platform to buy tickets. We were stranded in the crowded station, when a man approached me and asked if I knew any "specialists" who could get things done under the table. He seemed to have a military travel order for one leader plus seven subordinates, which would allow the purchase of eight tickets altogether. I said, "Show it to me." I looked at the travel order and saw that it lacked the requisite official seal. In spite of this, I decided to try my luck. I joined the line of military personnel, and with the document (which later proved to be false), I approached the ticket window. Inwardly I trembled with anxiety as the cashier took the document from my hand and disappeared. But she returned and offered to sell me eight tickets. I was thus able to help the man and his family, as well as my own. Tickets in hand, we faced further difficulties. The trains were full and the conductors allowed no one to board, but for 100 rubles, space for four was miraculously found. Thus we left Samarkand for Kermine. Mother will tell about Kermine.

◻    ◻    ◻

*It so happened that we met at Dr. Abend's house a Polish sergeant, Stefan Jerzyna, who was visiting from Kermine. He took a liking to us and offered to claim us as his family. He was single. He would list me as his sister, Arthur as his brother-in-law, and our two daughters as his nieces. When I told him we did not have money to pay him for his offer, his reply was, "I am not doing it for money; I only want to help you." He promised to let us know when we should come to Kermine. He wrote down the names of his mother, his father, and the church where Arthur and I were supposedly married. To memorize the names of my new "parents," the church, and the priest who "married" us was painful.*

*After a couple of weeks we received a note from Mr. Jerzyna asking us to come to Kermine.... The morning after our arrival, Jerzyna dropped by, brought us some food, and said, "We were betrayed." Betrayed?—by whom? Supposedly the Polish recruiting office got some hints about the bribes being taken by the soldiers and officers. But in the case of Jerzyna, would this kind-hearted man who had done so much for us without a penny, be punished? Later on that day we were called to the military army base. One of the officials asked me about my parents and my wedding. I dutifully gave all the answers I had memorized. Suddenly a Polish soldier rushed into the room, took Arthur, and told me to leave with the children....*

*The soldier took Arthur to the police station. After four hours of interrogation, Arthur had to admit our true identities, and they released him on the condition that he leave Kermine immediately. That same evening we tried to get train tickets, but it was impossible to obtain them because of the crowds coming and going from Kermine.*

*We went back to the small room which we had shared with three strangers. At 4 a.m. Arthur disappeared without saying a word. I had no idea where he went or what was on his mind. I was only waiting for his return in desperation and fear. At 11 a.m. he came back.*

*There were two separate Kermines, a village and a town, four miles apart. In both places were Polish recruitment centers. We were in Kermine village. Arthur went to the town of Kermine and walked into the military base. He asked for an interview with the man in charge, a high-ranking officer. Arthur told him that he was an engineer and a loyal Polish citizen, and asked if he could be of any*

*assistance.... The officer informed Arthur that this matter was not in his*

*jurisdiction but in that of his comrade, another high-ranking officer. Arthur went*

*to see the second officer and said that he was sent by the first one. That was not*

*true, but it made an impression on the officer. He asked Arthur for his wife's first*

*and maiden names. When Arthur answered, "Dora Gross," there was a moment*

*of silence and consternation.*

*"Is your wife Jewish?"*

*"Yes," answered Arthur. The officer asked another official, in French, what he*

*should do with this problem. Arthur understood their conversation. The other man*

*who was asked for advice stated that sometimes Polish men married Jewish girls.*

*The officer was satisfied with this answer and gave Arthur an exit permit to Iran.*

*Iran was a transit country for Polish military families on their way to Africa.*

*They never asked Arthur about his religion. Maybe because of his appearance*

*and the Polish-sounding name, he seemed a "true Pole" and they did not suspect*

*that he was Jewish. I looked with disbelief at the little slip of paper with these four*

*words, "Exit permit to Iran," which opened up a free world to us.*

*Our next destination was Krasnovodsk, a seaport on the south side of the*

*Caspian Sea in Soviet Russia. After eight hours we arrived there. Hundreds of*

*people were waiting for the ship which was to transfer us to Pahlavi,[11] the principal*

*port of Iran on the Caspian Sea.... A small ship arrived. I could not imagine how*

*this small vessel could carry hundreds of people across the Caspian Sea. People*

*started to get aboard. Some of them threw away suitcases too heavy to carry. They*

*pushed each other, hurrying and afraid of being left behind. We were not allowed to*

*take money into a foreign country, so we left the remaining few rubles with the*

---

[11] This port is now called Anzali.

*customs officials. The short voyage from Krasnovodsk to Pahlavi was a nightmare…. There was only one restroom for hundreds of people, and it was on the lower deck. We had to wait a long time for our turn. The adults could wait but not the little children. The mothers held them over the railing so they could relieve themselves. On two occasions the children slipped out of their mothers' arms and drowned. One could hear the screams of these distressed mothers. We were on the upper deck. When our little Zosia had to go to the bathroom, Arthur, holding her in his arms slid down a pole to get to the lower deck. Two older people died on this three-hour trip…. It was pouring rain when we arrived in Pahlavi.*

I have another story which belongs in the miracle category. In Tehran I reported to the military and was accepted. I would not be carrying a gun, but nevertheless I would be in the Polish army. I was scheduled to join the army in a few days. During this time, I happened to visit a friend, Bronek Fryling, at an agency of the Polish government-in-exile. Bronek was addressing me as "Mr. Engineer" (a common form of address in the Polish language), just as a Polish army major walked by. He overheard, and asked me "What is your engineering specialty?"

When I told him I was a civil engineer, he said, "That's splendid; we need civil engineers!"

"For what reason?" I asked.

"Because," he replied, "Polish citizens are being taken to Africa and we need to build camps for them."

I told him that I would be happy to go, but I was due to report to the army. He replied, "Oh, it's a small matter. I can get you out of that, on the condition that you agree to leave tomorrow."

"The difficulty," I said, "is that my wife is in the hospital with a high fever." He reassured me that she would have a nurse and a private railcar compartment. So it came to pass that instead of joining the army I found myself on the train bound for Ahwaz, Iran as deputy to the official in charge of the transport.

Ahwaz was the hottest place I had ever been. The heat was unbearable, with no relief night or day. I suffered from jaundice, Zosia from an eye infection. The misery lasted a month, but we came through it. Then we were transported by train to an Iranian port city, where a Dutch ship would take us to Karachi. Because of my knowledge of English, I was the official translator, and as such was given two first class cabins for me and my family and enjoyed many privileges including dining in the restaurant with the ship's officers. Among my tasks was translating between patients and doctors; patients' complaints in Polish, doctors' suggestions in English, for which my language skills were somewhat limited. It was not easy. We arrived in Karachi, where once again we were placed in a camp behind barbed wire. We waited there for a month for a transport that would take us to Mombasa and from there to the refugee camp in Tanganyika, where we remained for nearly six years.

# 5. BARTERING AND BRIBERY IN UZBEKISTAN: TALES FROM DUNIA AND MOTHER

In 1942, an estimated million Polish and Soviet Jews were living in Uzbekistan. Samarkand, Uzbekistan seemed to many refugees like a haven compared to Siberia, but many succumbed to illness.

Dunia's stamp collection survived the journey

Shortly before we left Tavda, a boy who liked me (it wasn't mutual) gave me three gifts that I put in my dress pocket: a pen knife, a pretty barbed fish hook—which embedded itself in my side and caused me considerable discomfort—and a pearl necklace. When I found out later that the pearls were real and belonged to his older sister, who was looking for them, I was afraid to admit that I had them, but also afraid to have them on me as we traveled. When we arrived in Samarkand, Uzbekistan, I buried them in the orchard under an apple tree, and marked the place with sticks. I have always wondered if anyone found the pearls and recognized their value.

In Samarkand we lived in a one-room hut in a compound which belonged to an Uzbek family. They also owned an apple orchard, as well as some donkeys and sheep. There must have also been cattle, since I recall how the family gathered cow dung and formed it into patties, which were used as fuel as well as plastered on the outside walls of the compound for insulation.

The Uzbek family consisted of parents; a 15-year-old daughter, Sadat; a 10-year-old son, Bahri; a new baby; and an old grandmother. Their huts were similar to ours, but in the center of their main hut there was a brazier around which the family sat on oriental carpets warming their feet. On top of the brazier was a low round table on which they had their meals. When the mother wanted her son to come to supper, she would call out in a sing-song voice, "Bahri, oh Bahri."

Sadat was a beautiful girl whose long hair was plaited into many tiny braids. When I asked her how many braids she had, she did not answer, but when I started to count them she ran screaming to her grandmother, who had to redo her hair. Apparently it was bad luck for anyone to know how many braids a girl had.

The crib in which the baby slept had a hole in it which was connected to an earthen pot below. The baby was placed with his bare bottom over the hole, and a round stick between the baby's legs was used to hold him in place, thus eliminating the need for diapers.

While we were there, the grandmother died, and the family hired a number of mourners who came every day for forty days, singing sad dirges. To feed the mourners, the father slaughtered a sheep which was roasted in a huge vat over an open fire.

I don't remember going hungry in Samarkand, but our diet was very meager. Once when Zosia and I were alone, I made potato soup— with no recipe or prior experience—and my four-year-old sister pronounced it the best soup she ever ate.

To supplement the small income from Father's job, I was designated to sell some of Mother's finery, such as silk nightgowns, satin pillowcases, etc. I also collected old bottles to sell. I had to trudge several miles through narrow streets and alleys of the old town to the open-air bazaar where I would spread my wares and bargain with the would-be buyers. Somehow I knew what the items were worth and how much I could get for them and I almost always got my price. Sometimes, I could use one or two cents to buy candies to sweeten my tea.

After each visit to the bazaar, I walked back, clutching my hard-earned money, and, miraculously, I was never accosted or robbed on these errands. I was a short, skinny twelve-year-old girl alone in a big foreign city, and yet it never occurred to me to be afraid or to feel that the task was too difficult or dangerous.

While we were in Samarkand, Father became ill with typhus, an illness with a very high mortality rate. Along with the telltale blotches on his skin, he ran a very high fever, had hallucinations, and lost consciousness. I was scared of his delirium. Mother had bought a pound of sugar on the black market to sweeten his tea. I took a sip of his tea, and he started screaming and crying that I'd poisoned myself. It was likely the delirium screaming at me, since typhus is passed by lice and is not contagious in this way.

◻︎    ◻︎    ◻︎

*Alexander 'borrowed' a bed from the hospital so that Arthur should not lie on the floor.[12] By this time Józia had succeeded in removing all lice and nits from the rest of the family. Otherwise all of us would have been infected.*

*It was forbidden to keep a person with a contagious disease at home. Spotted typhus had reached epidemic proportions among the refugees. Sanitary officials would remove whole families from their homes and put them in the few overcrowded hospitals. The death rate among the hospitalized refugees was alarming. I knew that if they put Arthur in a Samarkand hospital he would not survive. On the other hand, I needed a certificate with a diagnosis of another disease to present to his employer. Absence from work, in a Russian government enterprise, without excuse, meant prison.*

*We had a good Polish friend who was a physician working in a hospital. I turned to him for help. Dr. Abend advised me to go to a Russian doctor in charge*

---

[12] Alexander was at this point living across the road from our family and working at the local hospital.

*of all physicians in Samarkand and put 100 rubles on her desk, telling her that my husband had pneumonia and that I needed a certificate stating that fact. If she decided to come and examine Arthur I should give her another 100 rubles.... With much trepidation, I went to the doctor's office. She took the 100 rubles, gave me the certificate, and promised to come and examine Arthur. She came every day, got her money every time, never touched Arthur, and diagnosed the disease as pneumonia.*

*The crisis in spotted typhus comes after twenty-one days. The very high fever drops suddenly and the heart cannot take the sudden change. The patient dies unless the heart is continually stimulated. The Russian doctor told me, never mentioning the crisis, that she was not coming anymore.*

*But Dr. Abend came every day. He was only afraid he might meet the Russian doctor. We took precautions: Józia stood guard in the front of the hut so she could give us a signal through the window. There was one narrow escape. One day when Dr. Abend was there, we got the signal. Immediately he hid behind the dresses hanging on the line, and I stood in front of him, covering his protruding shoes.*

*On the night of the crisis, Dr. Abend sent us a trusted nurse, whose duty was to check Arthur's pulse all night. I sat on the floor close to her watching the expression on her face. At five o'clock in the morning, she exclaimed, "Things look bad," and her voice sounded urgent. Alexander ran for Dr. Abend, who lived not far from us. Within a few minutes he came, started frantically to pump morphine into Arthur's veins, and kept it up for two hours. Around seven o'clock he announced, "he will live." Dr. Abend was concerned about possible brain damage, one of the serious complications of spotted typhus, and the next day he brought two Polish neurologists for consultation. They examined Arthur and found him all right.*

*Dr. Abend not only saved Arthur's life, but also, by stealing morphine in small batches from the hospital, risked his job and imprisonment. The second person who helped me during Arthur's sickness was Alexander, the only one who was able to lift Arthur's inert body, open his mouth and pour in some liquid nourishment (tea) with a lot of sugar and wine. To obtain the sugar and wine, I had to take many risks. A neighbor gave me an address in a shady part of town where the black market was operating. We had smuggled in a few gold dollar coins,[13] and those constituted our assets. After the exchange on the black market, I was able, first, to pay the Russian doctor and, second, to buy the sugar and wine.*

[13] American gold eagle coins were hidden in a false bottom of a suitcase.

# 6. JÓZIA: THE UNSUNG HEROINE

It was common for Jewish middle-class families in Poland to hire Catholic nannies and housekeepers, but to have one support the family throughout a perilous, three-continent journey was definitely out of the ordinary.

Józia and Zosia in Tengeru

## Józia in Dunia's Life

Józia was a godsend. She came to us as a nanny, maid, and cook when I was about two or three and remained with us through all the trials of job losses, economic reversals, and finally the war and deportation. When money was scarce and my parents could not afford to buy me a new doll for my birthday, Józia spent her own money to buy a new head for my old doll and stayed up many nights making a doll wardrobe so it looked like a fancy new doll.

Incidentally, Mother told me much later that when they could not afford to pay Józia, as Father had lost his job, she said, "Prosze Pani,[14] kto mówi o pieniadzach?" (Please, who said anything about money?)

Józia always made me feel welcome and never lost patience with me. At Christmas she let me help her make cookies and we decorated a little Christmas tree with the cookies, candles, and homemade paper chains. That may have been the beginning of my lifelong love of Christmas trees. When walking, Józia would always find "treasures," and I learned to imitate her. To this day, I always look down when I walk, hoping to find loose coins, etc.

As an anxious response to my father's strict discipline, at the age of six or seven, I started throwing up at night in my bed. Józia, who had to wash my bedding, told me one day that I would have to start washing my own sheets. Miraculously, my nightly vomiting stopped. However, I also threw up regularly at dinnertime. Father's way of

---

[14] In this usage, Pani is similar to madam, a term of respect. The Polish word Pani is also used together with a first name (Pani Klara), with a title (Pani Doktor), with a last name (Pani Moszkowska). The male form is Pan, as in Pan Inzynier (Mr. Engineer), or if the engineer is female, she is Pani Inzynier. The wife of an engineer is Pani Inzynierova.

dealing with it was to punish me by taking away a favorite toy. When all the toys were thus confiscated and the vomiting continued, he threatened to start giving the toys away. Every day I lived in fear of dinnertime, with my anxiety growing hourly until the dreaded moment. Mother could not stand the tension so she left town to visit her father. Again, Józia took matters into her own hands. One afternoon she arranged a party for me, invited a couple of my friends and served all my favorite foods. I did not notice that dinnertime had come and gone. I never threw up at dinner after that. (It's amazing that Józia with her second-grade education knew more about child psychology than my highly educated parents.)

Józia always wore plain dresses. When she was given a gift of nice clothing, she would put it away in a trunk and call it her "trousseau." I am not sure if she had any dates, at least none that I remember. She did have a son out-of-wedlock, a likely result of improprieties by her former employer, who upon discovering her pregnancy promptly dismissed her. They also gave a negative recommendation, which Mother disregarded and hired her anyway. This may have been instrumental in Józia's devotion to us. One certainly could not find a more loyal, trustworthy, and loving person.

Józia's son lived with her mother in their native village, and she saw him only occasionally. It's always been a source of wonder to me that she chose to come with us and share our uncertain lot, instead of staying with her family.

Incidentally, the subject of Józia's son became a topic of conversation between a girlfriend and me when we were about eight years old. Her physician parents told her that two parents were needed to produce a baby, but I produced Józia's son as proof that it wasn't so and won the argument.

Józia doted on Zosia. From the time she was born, Zosia was "her baby." She sang to her, played with her, and cuddled with her, and Zosia adored her.

## Józia in Zosia's Life

From the time I was born to the time she got married and had a little girl of her own, Józia was the most important person in my life. In Poland, she was cook, housekeeper, and nanny. During the chaos of my early childhood, she was more a mother to me than my biological mother.

I don't know how I know that Józia held me and sang to me in the back of the truck during our escape from Radom, but my first distinct memory of Józia was in the ship on the way to Karachi [from Iran]. I was snuggling with her in the cargo hold that was packed with people and their belongings. It must have smelled pretty bad, what with all the unwashed bodies, but I was not cursed with my super-sensitive nose at that age. I remember that it felt so cozy and comforting to be there, away from the lonely, sterile cabin where the rest of my family was ensconced. Father was the official translator between the English crew and their boatload of Polish refugees, and as such he and only his immediate family were entitled to a cabin. I was not yet five, but I sensed that Józia was not happy to be in the cargo hold. I couldn't understand why.

This was the beginning of a rift between Józia and Father that would never heal. For a few months, we were all still together in a single hut in the refugee camp, Tengeru. I remember coming "home" to Józia in tears because I had scraped my knees or been teased. She was always there and she knew how to make the pain go away.

Then we moved to a pair of new huts, and Józia did not come with us. I continued to go to her. In retrospect, it seems that she always had freshly baked bread. She made me my favorite treat–butter and chopped onions on fresh bread. I would return to my family reeking of onions. Incidentally, Father hated onions.

I visited Józia a few times after she got married and had a baby, but it was not the same. I felt awkward around her husband, and now she had others on whom to lavish her love and attention. Soon, Father and I left Tengeru to live in Dar es Salaam. I never saw Józia again. Even many decades later, the remembrance of losing Józia still brings tears to my eyes.

I have often wondered why Józia did not stay in Poland when the Germans came. She was a Polish country woman and a Catholic. At the time, Hitler did not appear to be a threat to her.[15] Reportedly when Mother asked Józia why she chose to abandon her son to come with us she replied, "These are my children," indicating Dunia and me. Was that the only reason? We will never know. Instead of returning to her native village and her family, she put her very life on the line to share our hardship and uncertain fate. I doubt we would have survived the exodus without her.

---

[15] Hitler did later kill Polish Catholics, but in 1939 people thought only Jews were at risk.

# 7. A CHILD IN TENGERU: ZOSIA'S STORY

Tengeru was a Polish refugee camp in what was then known as Tanganyika (now, Tanzania) at the foot of Mount Meru, and near Mount Kilimanjaro in East Africa.

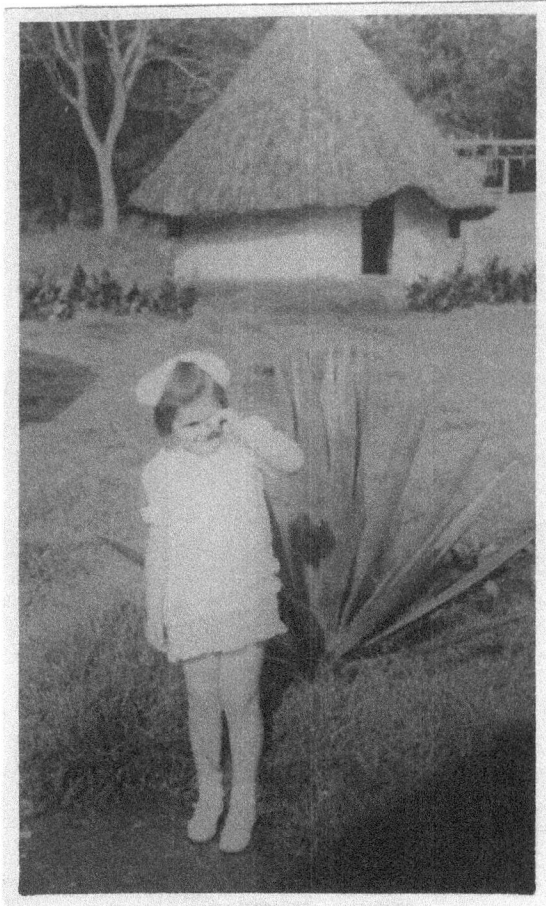

**Zosia in Front of a Typical Tengeru Hut**

When we first arrived in Tengeru, all five of us–Mother, Father, Józia, my sister, and I–lived in one small, mud-walled hut. All huts had conical banana-leaf roofs and packed earthen floors. I was subject to many knee scrapings at that age and remember that Józia was always there to comfort me. Later, after a fall-out between my father and Józia, the four of us moved about a block away to two adjacent huts. I missed Józia dreadfully and spent more waking hours in her hut than in ours.

Photo of Watercolor Painting of Our Two Huts

As camp engineer, our father was a big "bwana" and was allowed to hire an African youth to help us, as needed. After a while, one of our huts had a cement floor and the two huts were joined by an enclosed passageway. The hut with the cement floor was our living room by day, and Father's sleeping quarters at night. The other hut held three beds, one each for Mother, Dunia, and me. Each hut had a door, and on the wall directly opposite, a window with no glass pane.

There were no ceilings. In addition to our "hallway" and cement floor, we had another luxury—electric lights, which shone nightly during the two hours the nearby outdoor movie theater was showing films. Father jerry-rigged a connection to the electric generator; as far as I know his right to do this was never questioned by the authorities, and naturally there was no safety inspection.

Photo of Watercolor Painting of Our Garden

Our primitive home was surrounded by a lush garden. Father always loved plants and flowers and, with the help of young African men, put in an extensive array of plants. There was a hedge all around the property, a row of banana trees, a few papaya trees, a mango tree in the middle of a grassy area in the back, a large fragrant datura in front, and numerous flowering plants including cannas, primulas, and carnations. The garden was maintained by a teen-age boy, with whom Father communicated in Swahili. Swahili was the eighth in a series of languages Father had learned. He was fluent in Polish, German, and

English, well-versed in Russian, and was able to understand and make simple conversation in French, Italian, and Hebrew.

We were one of the few intact families in Tengeru. Most of the huts were occupied by women and children whose husbands and fathers were somewhere in Europe or North Africa fighting in the war. We were also among a tiny Jewish minority within a population of more than four thousand Polish Catholics. Many of these people were poorly educated and firmly believed that Jews killed their beloved Christ. One of the anti-Semitic myths they brought with them from Poland was that Jews killed Catholic children and used their blood in the making of matzos for Passover. Our family paid a price for what we were and what we had, each of us in a different way.

My parents were not religious but they clung to their Jewish identity and to a few traditions. Father was allowed to build a small synagogue. I remember going there with my parents (Dunia refused to go) for Passover. It was not a joyous occasion. The small congregation, mostly older single men, intoned in Hebrew for hours before anyone could eat. Mercifully, I was excused from the table, but not before I had become thoroughly bored and restless. There was little to do and no one to play with. I did, however, enjoy the matzos and sips of sweet wine.

The other religious observance I remember was Yom Kippur, a day dark with sorrow and marked by the eerie glow of a single large candle. This was the day my parents mourned those who had perished in the Holocaust, and the day Mother wept at the memory of her own mother's untimely death. I imagined the spirits of the dead drawn to the Yom Kippur candle, and I was terrified of it. Moths were drawn to the candle, and I developed a moth phobia which plagued me for over thirty tears.

The Synagogue Father Built

I had my fifth birthday in Tengeru and left the camp before my tenth. I cannot draw a map of the camp, but some things I do remember. Huts were organized into blocks with open spaces in between. There were fields of corn within the open spaces. I don't know who owned these cornfields, but I, and other children, used to pick fresh corn ears and roast them over an open fire.

In each block there was a community kitchen and dining area. This is where I learned to hate fatty, gristly meat, which Father insisted I eat. This is also where, on their own, some of the women baked wonderful bread and pastries using their elbows to test for the correct oven temperature. I remember Pani Kara, who managed to make

French pastries, especially her mouth-watering napoleons and cream puffs. Many in the camp kept chickens, mostly for eggs, but also for occasional slaughter on special occasions.

As it would have been in Poland, nobody worked on Sunday. After morning mass, the adults mostly sat around in the finest of their meager wardrobes. Sunday dinner from the communal kitchen was cold macaroni cooked on the previous day, and freshly made cottage cheese which we brought back to our huts. When sprinkled with sugar and cinnamon, this was by far my favorite meal of the week.

Our two huts were at the edge of our block. From the back yard the terrain sloped down into a valley, in which the outdoor theatre was located. On one side, a path led down through an empty field, then sloped up toward the next inhabited area. Once I started first grade, this was the path I trod every day. It went past an orphanage for boys, and then wound its way through a block of huts before ending at the school building. On the other side of the valley there was another path. I remember processions of mourners clad in black, keening and weeping, as they made their way down this path to the cemetery. It gave me the willies.

Footpaths connected huts and blocks, but there was one main dirt road in the camp to accommodate delivery trucks and an occasional bus or automobile. These vehicles would raise huge, choking clouds of dust as they passed by. The road led to the hospital. I was taken to the hospital a few times, either because of recurrent ear infections or toes inflamed by parasites. What I remember most about these visits were the flush toilets. I used to flush them just for the fun of it.

Within each block of huts there was a communal outhouse–a dark, smelly, fly-infested building, with several open stalls. In each stall there was an opening in the cement floor over which one had to squat. The stench was nauseating and I was always a little afraid of falling in. There was no toilet paper. Those lucky enough to have some old newspaper used that instead.

I was too scared ever to go to the outhouse after dark, when it was necessary to bring a lantern or to admit to Father that I was scared. Once night fell, I was allowed to pee in the dirt outside the hut, but sometimes I had to do more than pee. At those times I held it in, though it caused me considerable abdominal pain.

There was a water tap not far from the outhouse, where people traipsed with buckets to bring water back to their huts. For the most part, personal hygiene was rudimentary. However, unlike other refugees, our family had a warm bath once a week. Father got hold of a large empty oil drum, which our house servant filled with water and which was rigged up over an open fire. Warm water flowed by gravity into a bathtub set up in a small shack in a corner of the backyard. Mother had her own nightly cleansing ritual which puzzled me greatly; squatting over a basin of water, she would scoop up handfuls of water to wash between her legs.

My constant and best friend in the camp was Marta. Marta lived with her older sister, mother, and grandmother in the two huts closest to ours. Her Catholic family were Christians in the best sense of the word. They were not swayed by bigotry. Marta's grandmother, "Babcia" to many of us, often read us stories and fairy tales. As far as

I know she was the only one who read to children. Although their faith barred us from sharing Christmas Eve with them, every year they had us over for what I remember as a big feast on Christmas day.

Marta's mother, Pani Janka, slaughtered and prepared chickens for the Christmas feast and for other special occasions. I watched, fascinated, as she cleaned out the chicken guts; the things those guts contained! Lost rings, beads, even hairpins. My interest and lack of revulsion convinced my parents that I was destined to become a doctor. I adopted this goal as my own until my college zoology class, where I had to dissect a still warm, freshly killed, pregnant mouse. My stomach felt queasy, and I realized that test tubes, and not peoples' innards, were my destiny.

Early on there was a boy in our block who wanted to play with me, but he was a sissy and sometimes he messed in his pants. Marta and I ignored him, or ran away, or hurled insults, until he left us alone. I suspect he was Jewish, because Mother wanted me to be nice to him. Another short-lived neighbor and friend was a girl our age who lived alone with her mother. My parents disapproved of this friendship, and I sensed it had something to do with the many "uncles" who came to visit the mother. I don't know where my friend and her mother went, but they didn't stay for long.

A school was set up in the camp according to the Polish educational system. This meant that I could not start first grade until I was seven. For two years I went to kindergarten where the only supplies were paper and coloring pencils. I was terribly bored. When I finally started school, I was so ready that I absorbed the three R's like a sponge. I don't remember learning to read–just that all of a sudden I *could* read. Math and writing were equally easy. However, religious instruction was part of the curriculum and, infidel that I was, I was cast out of the classroom. I could roam freely for an hour, but I felt the stigma nevertheless. One day I returned a little early and saw the word "Moses" being hurriedly erased from the board. I felt confused; after all, Moses was "mine" too, so why was I sent away?

Actually, my first taste of discrimination came earlier. I was the only little girl in the neighborhood who was not invited to Halinka's sixth birthday party. I had thought we were friends, and I admired her greatly, especially for her dark, naturally curly hair. I had seen Shirley Temple in the "Secret Garden" at the outdoor theatre, and I thought curly hair was the epitome of prettiness. Oh, how I wanted to have naturally curly hair!

But the worst thing about being a little Jewish girl in Tengeru was walking to and from school. As I passed by, the orphanage boys would call me ugly names, laugh at me, and spit and urinate in my direction. The words and laughter reached me, but fortunately not their bodily missiles. Terrified as I was, I didn't tell my parents about this until much later when I was already an adult. Their response, "If we had known, we would have sent you away to a boarding school," confirmed how right I'd been to keep my mouth shut.

The only dogs in Tengeru were large ones, and I was afraid of them. Cats, however, were a different story. I loved cats ever since my first encounter with a mother cat and her kittens in Czortków. I don't know if I have faint memories of Trzy-Klopki, (three-dots) and her kittens, or if I'm relying on what I've been told. I was not quite two at the time. I very much wanted to adopt a kitten in Tengeru, but Mother would not hear of it. So I had to settle for a pet chicken, and later a pet wild duckling. The duckling and his brothers and sisters were hatched by an old hen inside a small enclosure Father built in the backyard. It's not clear how we came into possession of the hen or the clutch of wild duck eggs.

The night when the last duckling hatched we heard loud squawking and a lot of commotion from the chicken house. When we went to investigate we found, to our horror, that army ants had invaded the hen and her brood. The hen struggled to escape and, in her frenzy, squashed the ducklings until they were barely breathing. Marta's family came over, and we all tried to save the ducklings by holding them in the warmth of kerosene lamps.

In spite of all our efforts, only the first-hatched duckling survived. Covered with dark fuzz and bright colors on his head, he followed the hen everywhere. Then one day we placed him in a basin of water; he paddled contentedly while his "mother" clucked in great alarm. I'll never know what happened to my duckling. Our family went on a day trip to Arusha, the nearest town, and when we returned he was nowhere to be found. I was heartbroken.

At the age of eight I started piano lessons. The lessons were OK, but what I really liked was practicing. In a hut about a quarter mile from ours was an old upright piano, which was almost always available, since few took piano lessons and even fewer liked to practice.

Usually I was there alone, but on one occasion Marta was with me. Suddenly the door was yanked open and a woman with lots of red hair and a large dog rushed in, followed by a swarm of very angry bees. We all got thoroughly stung before the woman and dog rushed back out. As we ran home screaming, we saw the woman with her head under an outdoor faucet. I knew there would be no one home for me, so Marta and I went straight to her mother and grandmother, who proceeded to remove multiple bee stings from our heads, hands, and faces.

And then there was the memorable day, clear and sunny, when the sky turned dark with clouds. Not ordinary clouds, but huge swarms of locusts which blocked out the sun! As locusts rained everywhere, those with any sense barricaded themselves in their huts or other buildings. After the swarms moved out, I ventured outside and was amazed at the devastation. Plants had been decimated, and the cornfields laid bare.

# 8. COMING OF AGE IN TENGERU: DUNIA'S VOICE

There were approximately 4000 refugees in Tengeru, most of whom were Catholic. We were among the few Jews, and the only Jewish family.

Dunia and Zosia in Tengeru, 1942

When we arrived in Tengeru, three years after we had left Poland, I was twelve years old. I was small, with short cropped hair (after my head was shaved due to lice) and without any idea of what was in store for me. We found ourselves in a completely new and unknown territory at the edge of a jungle. We were housed in a round mud hut with banana leaf roof, dirt floor, and only mattresses with mosquito netting on the floor. Mother cried. We were free but away from any semblance of civilization or control over our destiny. The beginnings were not propitious.

Within days we started getting infected toenails, the result of some kind of soil-dwelling parasites which buried themselves under the toenails, laid their eggs, and caused painful infections. After a while we learned to remove the egg sacs without puncturing them. Strangely, in a short time they stopped bothering us.

We were warned not to go out in the sun without lined hats, to be wary of snakes (there was a dead python with a baby goat on display in front of the camp director's office), and not to drink the water without boiling it first. Everything around us, from the animals to the plants, was different from anything we had experienced. We had mangoes and papayas as well as bananas for the taking, though we talked nostalgically of crisp apples and juicy pears.

Gradually, we got used to the conditions. We moved to two huts, which Father connected by a passageway. We also slept in beds with frames for the mosquito netting, which was necessary to protect ourselves from mosquitoes as well as various insects that would fall from above.

Thanks to Polish ingenuity, a school was formed shortly after our arrival, Polish textbooks were obtained, and an amazing number of qualified teachers were found. The school was housed in barracks-like buildings. I started the sixth grade. I also made some friends.

My first friend was a neighbor girl named Janka, who had a younger sister who suffered from epilepsy. It was painful to watch and listen to her frequent grand-mal attacks. Janka and I started traipsing around in the jungle, seemingly fearless, though we dealt with our fears in typically childlike ways. Since I was afraid of snakes, and she of the natives, when a snake appeared, she would go first, and when we encountered natives, I would. We also drank the cool, fresh spring water despite all the warnings from adults. Amazingly, neither of us got sick.

One day Janka told me that she got something but would not tell me what. It was especially puzzling since she said she did not get it from anyone, and if I were more mature, I would know what she was talking about. I was not only not mature; I was completely ignorant of the reproductive system. I was also very naive and believed Janka when she told me that when I wasn't with her, all the cute boys would flirt with her. It made me jealous but not suspicious. (I guess I have always been somewhat gullible.) I don't know what happened to Janka after that, for they moved away and I never saw her again. Incidentally, when I did get my period at age fourteen, somehow I knew that it was normal, even though I was never told about menstruation, nor was I consciously aware of my knowledge.

After Janka moved out, a family moved in who became our lifelong friends. It consisted of the mother, Pani Janka Epler, her daughters, Basia and Marta, and mother-in-law, the beloved "Babcia," or grandma. Pani Janka became Mother's friend, a frequent visitor, and our bridge partner. Basia, at the time two years younger than me, was "just a kid," though over the years we have become quite close and have visited each other on several occasions. Marta and Zosia became inseparable, though their friendship did not continue beyond the camp.

My next friend was Alina, a peasant girl whose mother was illiterate. Since her hut was on the main road, we used to sit outside and people-watch by the hour. Alina was a fair student but seemed to excel in math. Only later did we learn to our great shock that she slept with our math teacher.

Eventually I moved up in my choice of friends. One of my friends was a studious, quiet girl named Lodka, and we used to take walks and talk. We also counted the number of steps between her hut and mine. When it was time to say goodbye, we would part at the exact middle of the distance. There was also Jadzia, another quiet girl, who was a good listener, as I liked to talk.

Then there was Theresa, a very smart girl and a born leader whom we all admired and tried to emulate. Theresa was a scout leader, and when her whole class staged a walkout in protest against a new English teacher (to replace my mother), Theresa tendered her resignation from Girl Scouts, believing that her insubordination violated the Girl Scout's code of ethics. (After the war, Theresa became a physician in England.)

Probably my longest lasting friends were Zosia Zadembska and Marysia Mosiewicz. But being in a three-way relationship, I often felt left out. They both played the piano. I was envious; I wanted to play but didn't want to practice. Marysia was in Tengeru without her family. When the Russians came to deport families from Poland, they took everyone who was in the house. She was visiting a friend, whose family was deported, so she went with them to Siberia and never saw her family again. She was in Tengeru with this family who ran a dairy farm. Still in Tengeru, she married an Englishman and moved to London with him. Zosia now lives in Leeds, England as a retired music teacher. I saw them both in London at a 1997 reunion of the Tengeru refugee camp.

All of my friends in camp were Catholic, and this difference caused me a lot of pain. I desperately wanted to belong and fit in, but being Jewish in an all-Catholic community was very difficult. There were only a handful of Jewish adults out of four thousand people, and my sister and I were the only Jewish children.

While I personally did not experience anti-Semitism, I knew that I would not be accepted into Girl Scouts, so I did not even try, but looked on longingly when almost all my friends had meetings and yearly Jamborees. I probably would not have had any dates, but that issue never came up, since most of the boys over the age of fifteen joined the junior cadets and left the camp. Consequently there were only six boys for some thirty or forty girls in my high school class. The other bone of contention that fueled the always present anti-Semitism was the fact that while most of the people in the camp were women and children (as their husbands were in the military), my father not only was present but also had all kinds of privileges as a camp engineer, such as having a house servant, a cement floor in the huts, and even electricity, which he rigged up on the nights when the movies were playing in the nearby outdoor theater.

This was also a time when Mother and I clashed over religion. Religion was never an issue before. My parents were not observant. In Poland all their friends were Jewish professionals, I played with their children, and religious matters were not discussed. In Russia the deportees were of both Catholic and Jewish background, and basic issues of survival were of primary interest.

But in Tengeru, along with my puberty, things came to a head. I wanted above all to fit in. I even asked a friend, if I learned to cross myself, would I be accepted? I did not want to be different; I wanted to be like everyone else. So I tried to conform to the norm. All my friends did their chores on Saturday and on Sunday would get dressed up and go to church. I tried to do likewise. Since one of my chores was the family laundry, I would do it on Saturday, and on Sunday would be all dressed up with no place to go. My mother took exception to that. She forced me to do the wash on Sunday, which I deeply resented.

Mother was proud of being Jewish and could not understand or accept a daughter who did not share her feelings. Once in desperation, I decided to run away from home. But I had no place to go; the camp was dark at night, and scary noises came from the jungle, so I meekly went back home.

At Christmas one year, I brought home a little branch (there were no evergreens around), stuck it in a pot, and decorated it with paper chains and homemade trinkets (as Józia and I had done in my childhood). It was a pathetic imitation of a Christmas tree but I was quite proud of it. However when Father came home and saw it, he bellowed, "a Christmas tree in my house!" and unceremoniously threw it out. I swore then and there that when I had my own house I was going to have a Christmas tree every year, and I followed through.

I don't remember what we ate in the camp. We had a communal kitchen that served dinner, which we had to carry to our huts. But I don't recall what we ate for breakfast or lunch. I do recall that our neighbor and friend, Pani Kara Pawluk, made the most delicious cakes by hand and baked them in the huge open fire oven, where she tested the temperature with her elbow. In any case, I gained quite a bit of weight and turned from a skinny child into a chubby adolescent.

When I reached puberty and needed a bra, Mother had a local seamstress make me some chest binding garments, which is what she wore before the war. I guess a girl was supposed to hide rather than show off her breasts. I also didn't know what to do with my hair, which was thick and straight. There were no mirrors in the camp, so other than occasional black and white photos, I didn't really know what I looked like. But still, I did not think I was attractive. Nobody told me about diets or fashions or how to fix my hair, and Mother was no help. Somehow she remained slender, while both Zosia and I became overweight.

I always did well in school. I was a conscientious student and tried to do my best. I excelled in Latin, Polish, and history. Math was a little harder, but my real downfall was chemistry. Under the Polish system, the last two years of high school were called a lyceum and were equivalent to college prep. School was compulsory through the tenth grade. Students who did not qualify for the lyceum could take vocational or business classes. At the end of the two years of lyceum, students had to take a matriculation examination in which they were tested in all the subjects over the past two years.

The Polish "matura" is a grueling experience. In Tengeru, good students were excused from some of the subjects. But because we were leaving the camp before the end of the school year, I was determined to take the "matura." I got a special dispensation from the Polish school authorities in Nairobi, and they sent a special examining commission to the camp for me. Needless to say, I was not exempt from any of the subjects. The subject I dreaded the most was chemistry. Mother even hired a tutor for me, and I tried my best, but I barely squeezed by in chemistry. I did well enough in the other subjects, and got my "matura" certificate. Even though I did it for my own satisfaction, it was that certification which, some two years later, admitted me to the University of California in Berkeley (after Professor Alfred Tarski translated my transcript). I even had a number of prerequisites waived. Ironically, my sister Zosia excelled in and majored in chemistry and eventually taught it at the high school level.

On the whole we were healthy in the six years in Tengeru, except for fairly frequent bouts of malaria, which, while not life threatening, had pretty unpleasant symptoms, such as chills and fever, headaches, body aches, etc. The camp doctors became quite adept at identifying the malaria symptoms, though occasionally they diagnosed other diseases as malaria. For the most part we were given quinine pills, which tasted awful and were hard to swallow. Another drug was Atabrine, which turned the skin bright yellow. This yellow skin lasted for about a week!

Once, however, I must have had a particularly virulent case of Malaria, because I was hospitalized. I was put on a ward with a number of other girls. In the morning a doctor came down the row of beds, giving each girl an injection in the bottom. I was terrified of shots and always screamed when I had to have one. This time I was in a dilemma. As one after another girl got her shot without protest, I didn't want to be the only one screaming. I didn't know how I was going to manage it, but I knew I couldn't scream. When my turn came, I turned over on my stomach, pulled down my pajama bottoms, and bit into my pillow. I did not scream then and thereafter stopped being afraid of shots.

There was a piano teacher in the camp and one piano for practicing. I took lessons for three years, but I'm sorry to say I did not make much progress because I hated practicing. Each student was allotted half an hour of practice and I kept looking at the clock every couple of minutes, waiting for the half hour to be over. What's worse was that my two closest friends were pretty accomplished pianists, having already taken lessons before the war, and I wanted to sound like them but without the effort of practicing. For a very short time I was also in the school chorus, but when the teacher found me holding my score upside down (I knew the words; I thought the notes were just for show), she reluctantly agreed with me that I was not cut out to be a singer. (She thought that everyone could be taught to sing.) Incidentally, not being able to sing the way I knew how it should sound has been my lifelong regret.

Another skill I tried to learn was sewing. Since Mother did not know how to sew on a button, she thought it would be a useful skill for me to learn. Unfortunately, the teacher had only one precious sewing machine, and if something broke she probably could not find the parts or a mechanic. So she was very reluctant to let the students use it. We did learn some basics, such as basting, hemming, and sewing on buttons, but that was the limit of my sewing education.

As far as the academic education was concerned, we had some excellent teachers. Mother taught English, and even though her own English was rudimentary, she was a good teacher, very fair and skilled in her profession. She inspired confidence and loyalty in her students, and I still get Christmas cards from some of them who tell me that Mother was the best teacher they ever had.

Our history teacher, who became the school principal and was Mother's good friend, was my personal favorite. She replaced another teacher while I was out sick one time, and I heard rumors about her being strict and demanding. As soon as I returned to school and heard her lecture, I decided that I would study extra hard to meet her expectations, and history became my favorite subject. This lady had a PhD, as did Mother and as did our Polish composition teacher. Our Latin teacher had been a lawyer, and while he knew Latin, his teaching methods left something to be desired. The math and science teacher was a brilliant man, but rumor had it that he had been shot in the head in the war, and that explained his rather erratic behavior.

My least favorite subject was P.E. Since we were usually lined up by height, being the shortest, I was either last or first. I was not very good at broad jumping and other gymnastic exercises, and was completely hopeless in volleyball. I probably have a rare distinction of being one person in the world who has never managed to hit the ball over the net in spite of trying hard to accomplish that goal. We also had a botany teacher who was a Girl Scout leader, and was dearly beloved by the Girl Scouts. She was well qualified, but I was not too fond of her. She was boring, but she was full of herself. The botany teacher was also jealous of my mother.

We called the teachers "professor" and stood up when they entered the classroom. Under the Polish system the students stayed in the same classroom, and the teachers were the ones who changed rooms. Most of the time we were quizzed orally and only rarely were there written exams. The exceptions were Polish compositions, and Latin translations. The desks were for two people. Since I was nearsighted and talked rather a lot, the teachers liked me to sit in front, hopefully with a quiet girl, but I am afraid I "corrupted" a couple of them.

# 9. FATHER: ZOSIA'S MEMORIES

Stories from Tengeru and Dar es Salaam, where Father remained true to his risk-taking nature.

**The family in front of our Tengeru huts**

Our father was a hero who saved our lives many times over. And, like many heroes he was, by nature, a risk taker. So it was that he often endangered the very lives he saved. Dunia, the first-born and, for seven years, only child bore the brunt of his adventuresome spirit.

When he was not immersed in his work, Father ruled the family according to a few simple beliefs. His was a black and white world in which things were either right or wrong. It was wrong to lie, no matter what the circumstance. It was right to give large sums of money to a relative in financial straits, wrong to spend pennies on ice cream treats. Father was a technophile, long before the word was coined. It was therefore right to buy the newest communications or computing device, wrong to pay for a restaurant meal. He had no patience for weakness or timidity. "No trespassing" or "keep off the grass" or even guard dogs were for the timid, and "my daughter is not afraid of…" was a phrase I often heard. He was angered by tears. He did not acknowledge emotional or psychological distress; and as for physical pain, there were two remedies–aspirin or castor oil.

My very first memory is of Father, the hero. I must have been about three years old. I was alone, standing at a train station. Then the train started to move. Looking around, I couldn't see any familiar faces and I was terrified. Suddenly, Father caught me up in his arms, and holding me securely, jumped onto the moving train. Mother and Dunia were already aboard.

There were few toys and no children's books in Tengeru. Two of my favorite pastimes when I was eight or nine were making "medicines," water extracts of colorful flowers and leaves, and collecting seeds of various kinds. With my growing pharmacy in mind, I was examining red berries which I picked from a tree in back of our huts when I was shaken by a thunderous voice, "Did you pick those berries?" Father was glaring at me. "No," I lied in fear.

"You are lying! I saw you do it," he bellowed in anger and then he spanked me.

I was furious at him. "You made me think you didn't know if I picked the berries, and that makes *you* a liar," I thought, but I didn't dare say it. Instead I ignored him for several days, during which I was especially sweet and loving toward Mother.

Father and I moved to Dar es Salaam in September of 1947, he to take on a real paying engineering job, I to go to school to learn English. There was a refugee camp in Dar es Salaam for Polish refugees and that was where we lived, in a single room in a barracks-style building topped by a corrugated metal roof. Inside were two bunk beds fitted with mosquito netting, a desk and chair, and a single lamp. In the evening, after a barely edible meal in the community dining room, Father would sit at the desk working on designs and drawings, oblivious to me and to the many insects flying around the lamp and his head. The door had to stay open in an attempt to cool the room that had become like a sauna from the tropical sun beating relentlessly all day on the metal roof. There was no screen door. These hours were the loneliest and most miserable for me. I had no friends, nothing to do, and no place to be.

In Dar es Salaam, British children had their own exclusive primary school. Native children did not attend school and everyone else, those of Greek, Indian, Dutch, etc. origins, were either resident or day students at a convent-run school. I was the only Polish refugee and the only one who did not speak any English. I was almost ten, and, except for math, was put back in first grade classes. This was total language immersion! I remember only two things about this learning process—one, I started by memorizing a science lesson on plants word by word, and two, I refused to speak English with Father.

Most afternoons after school, Father picked me up in the little two-seater convertible that belonged to his employer (driving to building sites was part of his job), and we went to the beach. I waited for him, wiltingly hot in my school uniform under the awning of an ice cream shop. My mouth watered for an ice cream, but I knew better than to ask. Going swimming was the only thing about our life in Dar es Salaam that I enjoyed. I loved the shell-covered beach, the buoyant refreshing ocean water, and the wind on my face as we drove.

On the way to the beach Father, feeling dutiful, tried to strike up conversations in his heavily accented English. "What did you do in school today, Sophie?" I either grunted or replied in Polish. After a day of struggling to understand and be understood, I very much needed to relax and be able to speak freely in my native tongue. Most of all I hated that he Anglicized my name! At first he got angry with me (the anger would dissipate once we got to the beach), but after a while he mercifully gave up the English lessons.

Father taught me the breaststroke, the only swimming method he knew. He had made an earlier attempt to teach me how to swim when we lived in Tengeru. There was a small lake nearby with a fishing pier from which Father threw me into the water, confident that I would instinctually be able to swim. Instead I tried to reach the bottom and spluttered, until he pulled me out; I was covered with leeches. There were no more swimming lessons in the lake.

In Dar es Salaam, wading in from the beach, I learned almost instantly, since it was so easy for me to stay afloat in the salt water. From the beach where we played and swam, we could see land across the bay. It didn't seem very far, so one afternoon Father decided I was ready to swim across. "Don't worry," he said, "If you get tired you can hold onto my shoulders."

We were about half way across when I got tired and started holding onto him. I had total faith in my father and was not scared a bit, even when he started breathing hard. We were drifting toward the open sea, when Father was able to grab onto a protruding mussel-encrusted section of a sunken ship. He rested awhile and then swam the rest of the distance to the opposite shore. His right hand was bleeding from holding onto the hull, but I still had no idea that we had been in any trouble.

"Are we going to swim back?" I asked.

"No," he said simply. We walked a distance, and then hitchhiked back to the swimming beach.

Then there was the castor oil incident. It took only one dose of castor oil at a very young age to teach me never to complain about a stomachache. But shortly before my tenth birthday, I had shooting pains in my abdomen that could not be denied. Sure enough, Father's response was a spoonful of castor oil. It was so vile tasting that I immediately threw up. Less than an hour later, I was rushed to the hospital in Dar es Salaam for an emergency appendectomy. Father threw out the castor oil. Had I not thrown up, the castor oil could have, and given the limited medical facilities in Dar es Salaam, probably would have, killed me.

# 10. JOHANNESBURG: ZOSIA'S VOICE

The system of apartheid reigned in South Africa during our family's stay from 1948 to 1950.

**Zosia on the porch of the Solsonia Lodge in Johannesburg**

Johannesburg was our fallback destination. We applied for a visa to the United States in 1945. This required a trip to the U.S. consulate in Nairobi, Kenya where we stayed for a couple of days in a hotel! We had a room on the fourth floor, and I was extremely impressed with the elevator and with how small people and vehicles seemed from that high up.

By 1948, with no visa in sight, our parents' hope for a life in the New World had dimmed, and the family needed to go where there were good engineering jobs and decent secondary schools.

When we first arrived in Johannesburg, we lived for a few days in a downtown hotel, which to me was very plush and luxurious. We walked along downtown streets past shops which displayed a dazzling array of goods, and took a bus out to a lake where for the very first time I saw, in the water, the myriad reflections of colorful lights. I was mesmerized. My other newfound delight was halva. One day when Mother, Dunia, and I were walking along the shops, Mother stopped to buy us this amazing treat which she remembered from her own days in Poland.

After the hotel, which we could ill afford for any length of time, we moved to the first of two boarding houses. The first boarding house was owned by a large, loud woman, in whom I saw a veritable storybook witch. I was very afraid of her. We didn't stay long, and I remember little else about the place, except that the toilet was outside and a long way from our single rented room.

I was glad when we moved to Solsonia Lodge, where we remained for the rest of our stay in Johannesburg. Here we had two rooms, actually more like a room and a large closet, one for our parents and one for Dunia and me. We ate in a communal dining room, where I discovered Jello and ketchup. I loved Jello, which was one of the few foods that did not require copious amounts of ketchup to make it palatable. From Solsonia Lodge I walked in one direction to school and in the opposite direction, along the base of a wooded hillside, to my weekly piano lessons.

Back in Tengeru, a visiting professor from the Krakow Conservatory of Music convinced Mother that I had musical talent. According to Mother, his exact words were, "Do not neglect this child." So she signed me up for lessons with a highly regarded piano teacher. I was actually taught by one of his assistants. Dutifully I walked to my piano lessons, a harrowing experience in the rainy season, when thunderstorms threatened and lightning flashed from the hill above my route. There was no piano at the boarding house, but somehow my parents arranged for me to practice next door in a house occupied by two elderly sisters.

I loved going over there, less for the piano than to sit in their elegant, lace-doily-enhanced parlor. I practiced daily, albeit without my earlier enthusiasm or enjoyment. If the women were aware of my frequent long breaks, they never breathed a word of it. I realized full well that I was not measuring up to my assumed potential, due either to lack of inherent ability, poor early training, more than a year away from the piano, or a combination of all three.

A few months after I started lessons, the great master was hosting a student recital. I was literally sick with anxiety. On the morning of the dreaded event, I developed severe intestinal pains which sent me to bed, groaning and moaning. Miracle of miracles, the following day, Dunia's birthday, I was completely well!

Doornfontein Primary School was a short walk from the lodge. I have a few vivid memories of school. One of these was the uniform I had to wear, a navy jumper and white blouse in the winter and a hideous lavender dress with yellow collar and cuffs in the summer. In sewing class, I learned to make very neat stitches by hand, and had a flannel nightgown to show for it.

In the fifth form (at age 11) I had a sadistic teacher who whacked students with a ruler at the slightest provocation. I was, at that time, a quiet and obedient student, but one day I made the mistake of writing my name on the top left of the paper instead of top right (or maybe it was the other way around), when "crack!" the ruler came down on my knuckles.

But worst of all, I had to learn Afrikaans on top of my still shaky English. It's an ungainly tongue, and I hated having to spend valuable time learning it. The other kids had been learning Afrikaans since first grade, and my parents hired a private tutor to help me bridge the gap. I took exit exams at the end of primary school and passed all subjects, including Afrikaans, with scores high enough to qualify for one of the two highest rated all-girl high schools in Johannesburg. I've often thought that it would have been a better fit for me than Willard, the junior high school in which I found myself in the United States. Incidentally, I forgot Afrikaans more quickly than I had learned it.

I wasn't bullied or teased at Doornfontein, but I wasn't very much befriended either. Except once at recess, when a pretty, dark-haired girl named Benicia approached me and asked, "Are you Jewish?" Weakly, I said, "Yes," not sure how she would react. But she smiled broadly and said, "So am I" and asked me over to her house. She and her family lived in a nice house a few blocks from school. I felt awkward. My life experiences had not prepared me to interact with a middle-class city girl, and I was ashamed that I lived in a boarding facility and had no home to which I could invite her. The friendship did not last.

There was a pear tree on the grounds of Solsonia Lodge. It was my place. I used to climb up into its branches, and sit and read, hidden from view among its greenery. When it was fruiting, I could eat pears right there in my perch. I remember one time when Mother was playing host to some poor soul and her 11-year-old son. The latter was foisted on me. Naturally, I assumed that he would enjoy climbing the tree. So I climbed up, and to my delight and disgust, he was too afraid to follow. "What a Mama's boy," I thought. Once again, my low opinion of boys was reinforced.

On warm summer afternoons Dunia and I used to walk to a nearby public pool, or rather a pool complex, which included a wading pool, a deep diving pool, and an Olympic size swimming pool. Like all public recreational areas in Johannesburg, and there were many, it was open to whites only and was maintained by native Africans who worked cheap and lived in shanties outside of town.

I turned eleven while living in the first boarding house. Strangely, I asked for and received a doll. I guess I was not ready to let go of my childhood and neither was my family, as they encouraged me in infantile games such as "Malinka lata" (the little one flies) as I leaped from bed to bed in our room. In fact, I didn't play much with that doll. Soon I had more serious things on my mind, such as pondering the difference between Judaism and Christianity and even questioning the existence of God.

There was a sizable prosperous Jewish population in Johannesburg. My parents were never especially religious, but they did attend services three times a year: Yom Kippur, Rosh Hashanah, and Passover. I remember going with them to a large, ornate synagogue, which must have been Orthodox, because Mother and I had to sit upstairs with the women, while the men gathered in the main room. The service was all in Hebrew, of which I did not understand a word. This was more than all right with me; I was free to indulge in my own thoughts, or to spend my time people watching and daydreaming. Mother, however, took my happy acquiescence as testimony to my "Jewishness." This was not unusual: both of my parents had a habit of ascribing feelings and motivations to me with little concern for their validity.

Looking back, I don't remember feeling any excitement, joy, or dismay when it was time to leave South Africa. It was just the next step on a journey that had not been mine to choose.

# EPILOGUE: COMING TO AMERICA

In 1950, the family arrived in America. We settled in California, where Mother and Father lived the rest of their lives and we (Dunia and Zosia) raised families of our own.

The family at our first house on Dwight Way in Berkeley, CA

## Zosia

Our family's final destination was Berkeley, California. Unlike the harrowing tales of other refugees to the United States, this part of our journey was unremarkable: train from Johannesburg to Cape Town, ship to South Hampton, a short stay in London, ship to New York and a cross-country train trip to Berkeley. I was stunned and dazzled by New York City, especially in contrast to London, which in the winter of 1950 still bore the scars of WWII and was dark, cold, and dank. The train trip across the northern United States was memorable for the winter wonderland scenes right outside the window.

Our arrival in Berkeley marked the end of an unlikely and highly uncertain journey, and the beginning of new stories of life in the New World. Many such stories have already been written. While each immigrant's experience is unique, we all share similar struggles as we assimilate into a new culture. I feel a kinship with countless others who have traveled difficult roads and overcome incredible odds to successfully establish new lives in America.

◻       ◻       ◻

## Dunia

When Mother and I left Tengeru in June 1948, we joined Father and Zosia in Dar es Salaam, from which we all traveled to Johannesburg, where Father got a job and I attended English high school. My mother's teaching had somewhat prepared me for the strange English in South Africa, and then in America. We waited in total five years for our American visa (a distant cousin in Berkeley got someone to sponsor the family).

We landed in New York City, February 1950, and Father's relatives met us; they offered a few days respite and sent us on to California, "the land of eternal spring," they said. My Aunt Sally took me to live with her in Houston to start college at the University of Houston while the rest of the family went on to Berkeley to get settled. At the end of the school year in June, Father had a job, the family had an apartment, and I joined them in Berkeley, where I enrolled at UC Berkeley in the fall semester, 1950 (I was later able to pay my father back every penny of the $150 tuition for non-residents).

Berkeley was a happy time for me: I earned my BA and Phi Beta Kappa honors and then my Masters in Social Work, I met my husband of sixty years, and we started our family.

Being a mother and a grandmother has been the focus of my life for the past sixty years. I have derived so much joy from watching my daughters and granddaughters grow up, becoming the amazing individuals they are.

# ACKNOWLEDGMENTS

This story has been a lifetime in the making. We would like to thank Ada's daughter Vicki Harrison and Sofia's daughter Julia Goldstein for their invaluable part in making this book a reality. We appreciate the conversations that helped jog our memories of events many decades in the past and the time they put in typing up sections from our mother's memoirs, editing our stories, collecting photos, and formatting the book.

We appreciate the roles our parents played: our mother for writing her memoirs and our father for recording his stories on tape, allowing us to channel their voices and combine them with ours to tell this family history.

# WORDS FROM THE EDITORS

## Julia

Editing my mother's and aunt's writing has given me the opportunity to understand their story better. Their anecdotes include those both familiar and new to me. I long knew, for example, about my mother's moth phobia, but never understood its source. Now I do. My mother had talked about Józia, the family's nanny and housekeeper, but I never grasped how important a role she played in my mother's childhood. I have a better understanding of my aunt's feelings about Christmas, coming of age in a primarily Catholic refugee community.

I had heard my grandfather was a risk taker, but I hadn't appreciated the extent of the risks he took, some brave and some foolish. I am grateful for the actions he took to save his family, and for the choices my grandmother made that may have seemed arbitrary at the time but turned out to be crucial. I am proud to have been able to work with my cousin to edit my family's story and share it with three generations of Moszkowski descendants.

◻     ◻     ◻

## Vicki

I grew up with the family story. It was dinnertime conversation throughout my childhood. As a UC Berkeley student living with my grandmother (Baba), I listened to Baba dole out portions of her story in response to whatever was going on in my life. If I was visiting my parents on a Tuesday night throughout the mid-1980s, when Baba was writing her memoirs, everything stopped at 7 p.m. for my mother's phone date with her mother. Back and forth between Polish and English, they remembered the details of their life, arguing in two languages whose version was the truth.

Assisting Julia as co-editor of our mothers' assemblage of the family story has been for me a joy and a fulfillment. We are, perhaps, a third layer of the telling, as we guide our family's words toward publication.

# ABOUT THE AUTHORS

The authors: Sofia (left) and Ada (right) in 2016

Sofia Moszkowski Freer retired from teaching chemistry and took up local politics in the early 2000s, serving on the planning commission in Half Moon Bay, CA. She now lives in the Puget Sound area with her husband Steve. Sofia has two daughters (Julia and Karen) and two grandsons (Alex and Dylan).

Ada Moszkowski Harrison is a retired Licensed Clinical Social Worker living in the San Francisco Bay Area, in the house she and her late husband Bill bought in 1969. She has three daughters (Diane, Vicki, and Heidi) and two granddaughters (Isabel and Leila).

www.ingramcontent.com/pod-product-compliance
Lightning Source LLC
Chambersburg PA
CBHW071637050426
42443CB00028B/3351